URBAN CULTURE DECODED

URBAN CULTURE DECODED

A Critical Analysis of the Physical, Mental, and
Spiritual State of a New Generation

THE BLACK DOT

MOME Publishing Inc.
New York, New York

For information contact:
MOME Publishing Inc.
1461 First Avenue, Suite 281
New York, NY 10075
844-HIP-HOP0
Email: urbandecoded@gmail.com

www.idecodeit.com
Facebook: urbanculturedecoded
Twitter: @theblackdot1
Instagram: idecodeit

Book cover design by Rasta Asaru Escott EL
Layout by Latonia Bowser

ISBN: 978-0-9772357-3-5

Printed in Canada

DEDICATION

This book is dedicated to the life, walk, and works of
Bro. AA Rashid.
You have opened my mind's eye to the spiritual connection
of everything in the universe.

HONORS

This book is in honor of my four children,
Marcus, Malcom, Elijah, and Odyssey.
This book is also in honor of my beautiful wife, Latonia Bowser,
my sister, April Johnson, and my nephew, Dandre Johnson.

CONTENTS

ABOUT THE FATHER

Some may ask, what qualifies me to write such a book? My answer is simple; these are the sum of my life experiences. These are the sum of the experiences of everyone who was born in an urban environment. While each individual person's journey may vary in degrees, we all shared a collection of experiences that became known as our life. Most urban environments were filled with the same challenges, drugs, violence, poverty, single-parent homes, food stamps, sexual misconduct and alcohol abuse. As children, we did not view these situations as challenges; this was just everyday life since we didn't know any better. We still went outside and played all day long, we still went to the pool, we still played sports, we still went to the jams in the park and we still went to school with a smile on our faces. Every child shared the same social, domestic and economic status so we didn't even know we were poor. We shared what little we had with our neighbors and friends; we got new clothes for the first day of school, Easter, and Christmas. The only white people that we ever came in direct contact with were our teachers, police officers and the social workers. There may have been one or two children who were doing a little better because they had their mom and dad in their lives, but not by much. They still lived in the same tenement building that we did. Every parent and elder on the block had the right to chastise or even whoop your butt if they had to. Then you got another beating when your moms came home! The community functioned as a community. Little did we know that these experiences were preparing us for urban warfare. In order to survive the urban terrain you had to be physically, mentally, and spiritually strengthened by these experiences. Little did we know that they were preparing us to deal with any and all obstacles that we would encounter without even missing a step or breaking a sweat. Pressure bust pipes, but it also creates diamonds, the diamonds are in the ruff, and the ruff is the urban experience in its totality. As a result, I would not change one single thing about my childhood, or the experiences that I have endured.

With that being said, it wasn't until I became a father that I realized that our condition was systematic. It wasn't until I became a father that I realized that our life was a complicated maze of trials and tribulations designed to keep us running in place, never truly experiencing anything outside of the maze itself. Unlike a normal maze with pathways leading to different destinations based on one's decisions, this is a complex maze where every decision you make could lead right back to where you started. The maze is literal and symbolic. There is a liquor store, church, Chinese restaurant, Planned Parenthood Center, and pharmacy on every corner of the maze. So every path looks the same when you enter it. The abuse of drugs and alcohol can make it very difficult to master the layout of the maze, hindering and rendering those who do so, useless. However, certain drugs, if properly used and understood, could eliminate the maze altogether. Remember, "There is no spoon." Then there are those who are physically able to escape the maze, using their talents as an athlete, entertainer, or hustler. Yet they still carry the mental imprint of the maze wherever they go, so they begin to rebuild the maze all over again as a continuation of the original one. We have all heard the saying, "You can take a brother out of the hood, but you can't take the hood out of a brother." Our personal experiences navigating through the maze help us develop a mental roadmap of its layout, but the maze changes every generation based on the consciousness of those trying to escape it. So the "path" that you took may not work for your children. One's journey into spirituality is a maze unto itself that requires navigational skills beyond the physical and mental understanding of things. Our youth are confused on so many levels. They are relying on us for the blueprint. They all want out of the maze. You can't just physically escape it. You have to mentally and spiritually be able to conquer and truly master it.

I am the father of three young men ages 28, 21, and 15. I also have a 13-year-old daughter, so the challenge of raising each child was different based on that day and time that each one was born. There was no set blueprint that could be used for all of them. A seven year difference is a lifetime in terms of raising children. As an 18-year-old dad, my first son raised me. I made a lot of mistakes being that my own dad was not around to guide me in the science of fatherhood. I didn't have my next son until I was 25-years-old, so he benefited from the experience of my previous mistakes. I was a bit more established and understood the importance of my presence in a young man's life at that time. I had my last son at 31-years-old and considered myself a pro by this time with many experiences that I could draw on to solve problems related to raising young men in particular. Here is where the string theory comes into play. Each child is used to help raise the next child. They are connected. The oldest brother sets the standard for the younger ones. Then there is my 13-year-old daughter who is the baby, but a different energy altogether. I use all three of my sons to teach my daughter the importance of her self worth by making sure that they treat all women with the utmost respect, as well as me treating her mother the same. With all of the external influences that control the lives of young girls, it is important that they feel sheltered and respected by the men that they trust the most. My 15-year-old son and daughter were raised in the era of social media as well, so my approach is different then it was with my oldest son who didn't even have a cell phone at 15.

As parents we need to be swift and changeable because the maze will change at an alarming rate. My experiences as a parent and tutor have given my valuable insight into what it takes to navigate the maze of urban America. When I couple this with my personal journey of roaming the streets from the tender age of 3-years-old, it provides me with valuable knowledge that can benefit all who read this book. However, this will be an unconventional approach. The conventional way of thinking only reinforces the maze's ability to keep us on lockdown. In order to unlock and decode the mysteries of this paradigm; it will require us to see things from a different perspective. The analysis of this book will be from multiple perspectives, as a parent, as a child who survived the urban experience, and from the eyes of those who are experiencing it today. So walk with me as a take you on a journey through an urban experience like you have never witnessed before.

FOREWORD

A book's composer is a slice of God. I know Black Dot. I'm honored to know him. I can die and say I met a saint. It's rare to meet a man who contributes as he does so selflessly. The true contribution however is this literary offering. Time determines the outcome of realities gifts of experience. These gifts are timely contributions to humanities required tutelage to advance as a collective species. Sound is the medium of change. Change is antagonized by great voices. Those voices which are connected to the nature of their environment.

Black Dot is from where Hip Hop manifested. His blood vessels are manufactured with the forces that healed impoverished hearts torn down by poverty. His bones are molded by the resonate frequency of survival. I trust his vibration. I love the artist who meets the people where they at. I met Black Dot in Prison. I was the prisoner and he was the saint who came in the valley of the shadow of death with a box of books, and accompanied by Reverend Phil Valentine, who spoke to about 350 prisoners. We will tell that entire story in a film. However those books left behind spawned a consciousness revolution that is still matriculating and manifesting. Black Dot heard Hip Hop first make its debut in the park. In the park the music resonated through the walls of Black Dot's home and healed the missing pieces of his and our American pie. Now Hip Hop is the leading means by which to unify humans. A child of poverty became the mitigating factor to determine the outcome of world peace.

When I read books, I explore a few factors. "Why?" is the initial question I ask. This book you are holding is for the purpose of enacting the psychodrama of the imagination and it's power and influence over human behavior. By creating a place to factor power objectively can we find force, and concentrating on form generates force. We often think that morality or consciousness or karma, or what ever you call the act of doing good, is the God of this universe. Of course that's not the case. With all of the apparent abuses inflicted on the innocent, we become aware that there exist forces that favor movements. These forces serve every one who knows their forms. Movements have forms and they have guides. Your morality is yours.

The forces you summon to live your morality belong to everyone. The travesty of being black in America is that it includes the impoverished experience of slavery. This experience unfortunately included intentionally making people ignorant of their origins. A people's origin is included in their cosmology. There cosmology constitutes their religious ideology. There cosmology offers instruction on how to manipulate the available forces freely given by the universe. Your soul's responsibility is to maintain control over the circumstances surrounding its existence. Hip Hop is a bridge made by our ancestors to assist souls to their healing. Even the trap rap crack rap swag rap are evidence of concerns to be addressed not souls to condemn. The right soul exists in the Black Dot. He is ready for this task.

In closing, I want to offer this to the reader who have an ear for wisdom. Man is a light being who vibrates and changes according to sound frequency. Listen to the words that you read as they psycho acoustically rearrange your frame of space. Sounds when heard find emotional centers to vibrate with and affect human behaviors. Various sounds have ancient archetypes associated to their function, which derives from several million years of human thought. These sounds are equipped with tones, which are associated with body parts and cellular structure as well as the stars systems. We are a bi-product of stellar sound. The Hebrew root for the word for Ear and Hear AZN is AZ:

Strong's Number H0227
אז 'az {awz} a demonstrative adv; TWOT - 54; adv AV - beginning, even, for, from, hitherto, now, old, since, then, time, when, yet; 22
1) then, at that time 1a) temporal expressions 1a1) then (past) 1a2) then, if...then (future) 1a3) earlier 1b) logical expressions 1b1) in that case 1b2) that (being so)

We find its use in
Genesis 4:26 as the word "began"
Meaning the big in in a sense means to hear. The book you are holding is yours and that's your voice reading the truths that belong to you. Genesis reads...

"And to Seth, to him also there was born a son; and he called his name Enos: then began men to call upon the name of the LORD."

Here we see the root of Hearing and Sound are the same word for beginning. The archetypes of logical deduction are as follows. We have the Aleph, which is the Primal will to be the OX, and the Zayin, which means sword.

We see this root is composed of two letters, the first Aleph and the seventh. Combined they equal the number 8, 8 being a symbolic key connecting our symbol literate mind to the commonly known musical octaves. Octave comes from the Greek Octavus meaning 8. An octave is a unit of measurement associated to sound. The language of old includes anchors upon which we hoist upon the shores of symbols to keep us safe from floating away with the chaotic current of individual and collective thought forms. The symbol literate mind of the seeker is involved with the cosmic destiny of manifestation, which accomplishes its ends through, mans thoughts. How many of us can find a guidebook of instruction along this journey? Each being on this planet is a vehicle. If it has the ability to perceive, its perception acts as the means through which matter is allowed to exist. Your child is creating a world and that world good or bad is being created by what you have offered in your words. The ones you speak and the ones you read and you write. And hopefully some of you will listen. Give Black Dot your ear. *Hear is your guide.*

AA RASHID, LOS ANGELES CALIFORNIA 2015

Words are triggers directing intent to your greatest fear or desire.

- Bro. A. A. Rashid

http://.aarashid.com

http://www.youtube.com/user/qabalagod

http://myspace.com/bro_aa_rashid

DISCLAIMER

W arning: this book will not be conventional in the sense that it will try to provide politically correct answers to the problems that we are facing in urban America. A subject of this matter requires a deeper analysis that goes well beyond the scope of one's typical way of thinking, so I wrote this book as a starting point in an attempt to address such matters. We must explore unconventional solutions, or at least view the situation from an unconventional standpoint if we want to make any true breakthroughs. If we are going to deal with the core of the problems that we as an urban society are faced with in regards to our youth, we must be open and honest about the current state that they live in. While it is important that we address the cause of the situation, it is also equally important that we look at the affects of living in an artificial environment plagued by violence, drugs, unemployment, discrimination, and police brutality. How could one not be violent in the face of all the violence that we have endured over the last 400 years? How could one not want to use drugs as an escape from all of the hardships related to living in such conditions? When faced with the option of being hungry and unemployed, or hitting the streets to sell drugs, how could one not make the choice of getting paid? This is a no-brainer when the concept of survival is on the line. The million-dollar question is, what if the same things that plagued us could save us? This generation has learned to embrace the unbearable. That old saying, "whatever doesn't kill you will only make you stronger" rings true with this generation. Drugs and alcohol, which have cause so much damage to the previous generation, has almost had the reverse affect on this generation. They have become immune to the negative affects. They have become stronger than ever before. They celebrate life in what appears to be the direst situations, leaving even their oppressors confused. They have created an entire culture based on the type of music that they listen to, the type of drugs and alcohol that they use, and their sexual behaviors.

While most will view them as violent, lost, and confused troublemakers with no regard for life, in my humble opinion, they are the most advanced, enlightened, and spiritual beings on the planet. They just lack the knowledge, wisdom, and understanding of who they really are. As a result, their actions are in contrary of such divine principles. They have bottomed out, and are now using the very vices that were meant to weigh them down, to uplift them. I call this urban alchemy. To the parents, teachers, and elders who have all but given up on this generation, and scoff at the notion that they are an asset, I have but a few questions to ask you, have you taught them about sex magic and the power of using their creative energy to activate their spirituality? Have you taught them about the use of certain drugs that could assist them in seeing beyond this so-called reality and their connection to everything in the universe? Have you taught them about the power of music and sound vibration, and its ability to heal and open up their spiritual centers? If you have answered no to any of these questions, then it is *you* who are out of touch with the current reality that they reside in. They are in the process of a metamorphosis unlike what we have ever witnessed before. If your response is, this is just some mumbo jumbo "new Age" nonsense, then it shows that you are really out of touch with the transformation that we are all making, which is being led by this cast of rebellious, misunderstood youth.

Some of you may have already put the book down, for those who are still with me, strap on your seatbelt because we are about to go on one hell of a ride. I too was looking on the surface at all of the problems that our youth were causing, until I began to look under the surface at what was really going on. Then it dawned on me: I wasn't witnessing the demise of a culture. I was witnessing the rise of a culture! Birth is violent, so to usher in a new paradigm will require an uncomfortable period in our history that will undoubtedly lead to a new paradise. We will have our youth to thank for it. However, to understand them, we must first understand the culture that bred them. So I present to you...*Urban Culture Decoded, A Critical Analysis of the Physical, Mental, and Spiritual State of a New Generation.*

INTRODUCTION

I wrote this book not to criticize or glorify urban culture, but to place it in its proper perspective in regards to its importance in today's society. We as parents have not placed enough emphases on the outside influences that have made it tough to raise our children in today's world. We believe that the values and principles that we have instilled in our children from within the home will be sufficed. Well, forty or fifty years ago this may have been true. That old saying "it takes a village to raise a child" has taken on a whole new meaning in 2015 and beyond. The sphere of external influence has increased exponentially making it extremely hard to raise and govern a child. So when I speak about urban culture, or Rap culture in great detail, please do not allow what you think you know about these subjects make you become dismissive or the negative connotations placed on the topics to lead you to the same results without due diligence. Urban culture is a way of life that has had a great affect on the thinking of our youth. Remember that ones actions are a direct result of ones thinking. So if we want to know why our children act the way that they do, we must first attempt to understand the source of their thinking. Hip Hop and Rap are at the root of this thinking, but this is not a book about Hip Hop. It is a Book about urban culture as a whole, which was birthed by Hip Hop. Hip Hop set the foundation, however, Rap, social media, drugs, violence, education, sex, and many other aspects have all become subcultures of the urban experience. These are the components of life that we who live in urban environments have to face and navigate through on a daily basis.

This Urban Culture that I will speak about in great detail has been engrained into the very fiber of our youth. They cannot escape it. We as parents, teachers and elders must have a greater understanding of what we are dealing with in order to combat the aspects of it that we do not like, and harness the principles that we appreciate. I believe that the current dropout rate, incarceration rate, crime rate, and unemployment rate amongst our youth is directly related to the influence of what has become Urban Culture. This is not to suggest that all of it can be attributed to the culture or that all of it is negative. We too have to bare the responsibility of raising and educating our youth. A large part of the problem can be attributed to our inability to morph and adjust our methods of teaching, communicating, and assimilating. We as parents and teachers have become outdated and rigid in our thinking when it comes to the challenges that this generation is facing. This culture has also created a communication barrier between parents, teachers and children alike. Dealing with today's youth is equivalent to traveling to a foreign country and not understanding the language, traditions, and culture of the native people. Parents and teachers, who have not taken the time to learn what the culture is about, misunderstand much of it. As a result, those who do not understand the culture have a biased view of the culture. And the media, school system, religious groups, etc. only see the negative results that it has yielded and has given up on this generation.

This generation is just crying out for help. Then there are those who have abused the culture for their own personal gains like corporations, shady music executives, and other greedy organizations. The results of this carnage will be well documented throughout this book as well. But in the end, what was once thought of as a passing fad (Hip Hop) has now permeated every fiber of American culture and abroad. It has crossed every racial, ethnic, and cultural line to become the universal language of the new generation. On one hand it has united more people than any Pope, Politician, Reverend, or Civil Rights leader in history. But on the other hand it has divided the youth and their elders. It has created a bridge between teachers and their students. The gap between society and its youth has never been greater. This body of work will attempt to bridge that gap by examining the affects of urban culture in our society in great detail.

CHAPTER 1

WHAT GOES AROUND

For those of you who are old enough to remember the sixties, it too represented a rebellious time for the urban youth of that era. There was police brutality, unemployment, discrimination, segregation, and poor living conditions. But there was also incredible music like Blues, R&B, and Jazz, which on the surface seems like a contradiction of sorts. But as you will see later, nothing could be further from the truth!

Marijuana and alcohol were the vices of choice during this era, and the protests for Civil Rights galvanized the people. Flash forward to the year 2015, and those same youth of the sixties are now parents who claim not to understand their own children. Yet today there is still police brutality, discrimination, unemployment, and poor living conditions. Today, the music of the choice is Hip Hop, Rap, and World music. The vices of choice are exotic blends of marijuana, ecstasy (molly), prescription drugs, and the abuse of alcohol is at an all time high.

Now, lets deal with the "elephant" in the room. Drugs and alcohol are synonymous with unemployment, crime, poor living conditions, and low education. They are also synonymous with music and art as a whole. We as parents and teachers may not want to accept this reality but it is just that…reality. As we begin to break down and examine urban culture we will begin to notice the same elements at play. It doesn't matter if you feel that they are right or wrong. It doesn't matter if you feel that they have a negative or positive affect on our youth or society as a whole, they are an intricate part of the culture. They cannot be separated. As much as we would like to deal with each problem individually, we must address the issue as a whole. Allow me to explain. When a child has a drug or alcohol problem the conventional method of helping the child would be to send them to rehab. But when the music that they listen to, the videos games that they play, and the movies and reality TV that they watch all promote the latter, rehab becomes a waste of time. These vices are accepted amongst their peers. It's almost like the culture itself is a gateway drug. The music in particular is a reflection of the heightened times in which it was produced. This is critical as we examine the blueprint of what urban culture in this day and time has become. Songs from love to revolution each play an equal role in the soundtrack of our lives. We use the art of the time to express our pain and struggle, whether it was Jazz, Blues, or Spoken Word then, or Hip Hop, Rap, or World Music today. Unfortunately, the same can be said about drugs, sex, and alcohol for that matter. The more heightened the tension, the more potent the drugs become to help escape the burdens of this reality.

Today that reality is further skewed by the many challenges that today's youth are faced with like bullying, peer pressure, gang violence, sexual orientation, just to name a few. This is not just subjected to urban areas, but urban areas are affected at a higher rate than most. On one hand, the youth will use this mixture sex, art, and drugs to help escape the current conditions in which they face, even if it is just temporarily, and on the other hand, these same vices become tools of their own destruction. The biggest communities hit, and usually from both angles are the urban sections. The lack of education and resources make music and drugs a viable second option. Whether we would like to accept it or not; music, drugs, and violence have become a part of the culture due to the external conditions that make life difficult in the inner cities and other poor neighborhoods. Some may see this as an excuse as to why our youth act the way they do. But history has shown that when there is an influx of jobs, education and opportunity; crime rates drop. When a people are constantly placed in survival mode, the results can and will be expressed in violent, criminal, and unethical ways.

CHAPTER 2

MUSIC

Music is the driving force of this new culture. It gives birth to all of the other avenues. The fashion we see, the products that are being marketed to us, and the overall commercialism of everything is a direct result of the music. The music promotes the lifestyle as well. Whether it's gangster music, hustler music, trap music, or sex music; the music is the law. When a song is played over and over again on the radio and the fans sing along, the words become a chant. When we chant with intent, consciously or subconsciously, we bring that which we are chanting about into existence. Now, the amount of people chanting and the frequency of the chant will determine the speed and rate in which the results will be achieved. Also, this process is further accelerated when the visuals are added via music videos, YouTube, etc. So think about the same song being played simultaneously across the country on a thousand radio stations and you can begin to see the affects of the music from a different perspective. This process can also have a positive affect if the music and visuals are positive, but have you listened to the radio lately? Corporations have found clever waysto take advantage of this science by paying artist to incorporate their products into the music.

The Prison industry has also profited from the violence and "get rich or die trying" mentality of our youth. And they too are a corporation! The education system has suffered tremendously because today's youth are more prone to skip school in an attempt to make music with the hopes of making it big. The many artists who achieve success without ever finishing high school further support this type of thinking. Most rap artists promote criminal activity as a means to get the start up money to pursue a career in music. Simply put, for this generation; music is God. At best, parents and teachers have to understand that music is a weapon and in its natural state, a weapon is neutral. It can be used for good (protect), or evil (kill). In the case of Hip Hop in the early eighties, we used it as a weapon of protest against police brutality, unemployment, and the many injustices that we were faced with on a daily basis. It was the only voice that we had at the time, so we expressed our frustration through dance, art, spoken word, and the drum. It temporarily relieved the pain. Just as our ancestors before us used music to escape the hardships of being slaves on a plantation, we too found solace in the muse. It became our insulation (protection) from the outside world. As you can see over the course of time, the barrel of the "gun" was pointed back at us and Hip Hop became a weapon of its own self-destruction. Eventually the music began to function like a mind control program that fueled itself. Each generation was, and is affected more than the one before it.

The vibration of music in general has devolved dramatically. Never before in the annals of time have the lyrics to songs been so vulgar. Never before have the lyrics been so violent. Never before have we so openly celebrated the degradation of women or the use of drugs. Under the guise of freedom of speech and "creative" expression, the envelope has been pushed to new boundaries without any true accountability. Artist hide behind these terms to deflect the fact that their words are causing harm to those who listen, especially young minds that are still being molded by their experiences. The music is critical because it has the ability to bypass the conscious mind and enter into the subconscious mind, even without your permission. So you can't fight off or ignore music, you can only make yourself aware of its presence and try to safeguard against unwanted subliminal messages planted within the music. The digital era in music has made it possible for those with no formal training in music to compose great masterpieces, but sometimes, the understanding of how powerful music is can be lost in the digital production and the automated translation of the producer. Digital sound is what sound would sound like if it were really sound. It is an interpretation of sound, using 1's and 0's as markers. By not actually playing instruments (in some cases), the spiritual process of using the physical body to enhance sound is bypassed. That's where the true magic of music resides.

The actual instrument is only an extension of the body, mind and soul of the musician. The jump from analog to digital in every aspect of our lives is critical because it symbolizes the thought process of our youth who want instant results from the efforts. I call it the "microwave" era. Or better yet, it should be called the "digital" era. They want to skip the linear process of achieving their goals. As fast as they can think it, they want to see it. They even have digital cigarettes out now, wow. Most parents and teachers are stuck in the analog way of thinking, which is played out. Our children are digital thinkers so we must upgrade our program or we become obsolete in their eyes. The music is the catalyst. My ancestors taught, "Music is the gateway to the spirit world". If this is the case we must protect the doorways in which energy is allowed to enter to ensure that hostile forces are kept at bay. But with so many uninitiated people creating music, dancing to music and being lost within the music, the process is easier said than done.

CHAPTER 3

HIP HOP IS THE FOUNDATION

For every cause there is an effect. If you eliminate jobs the effects will be higher unemployment rates, which will lead to higher crime rates. If you eliminate education, then the effects will be higher dropout rates, which inevitably lead to unemployment, which leads back to higher crime rates, etc. The history of Hip Hop began with the elimination of the music, art, and dance programs in urban schools. This may not seem significant unless you understand the importance of music, art and dance to black youth in particular. They are embedded deep within our DNA and have been a part of our culture for thousands of years. Traces of the muse have accompanied us throughout our worldly travels including our demise into slavery. We have found solace during the most wretched of times using music, art and dance as the primary outlet. Denying black people the opportunity to dance, sing, draw, or play instruments is like denying a bird a chance to fly. So when these programs were shut down, we were forced to create an alternate form of expression which would be later called Hip Hop. In the beginning, Hip Hop was composed of four components that we later called elements, the graffiti or aerosol artist, The DJ, The B-Boy and

B-Girl, and The Emcee. Each one of these elements can be traced back to our ancient ancestry.

What was once known as Hieroglyphics in ancient times has morphed into today's modern day graffiti or graphic artist. Some may find this to be a stretch because on the surface they are vastly different, but let's examine just how similar they really are. It has been said that a picture is worth a thousand words. Hieroglyphs are pictures, symbols, sigils and archetypes used to convey messages. Some tell stories while others may heed warnings or foretell of future events. The original graffiti pieces served the same purpose. They were socially motivated renderings placed on stonewalls, usually tenement buildings, or subway stations and trains. They were very colorful, very enigmatic, and had to be deciphered to understand their true meanings. The fact that graffiti has been labeled vandalism links back to the elimination of the art programs, leaving a void in the outlets available to express ones self through this medium. So pay close attention to the child that's always scribbling in his or her notebook. And as parents and teachers make it your priority to allow these creative juices to flow by providing the necessary tools of expression. The fact that hieroglyphs can be traced back to at least 3000 B.C. and had its origins in ancient Egypt (Khemet) should also be made known to the youth because it may instill a sense of pride in them, especially Black children since a lot of the text books in school seem to focus on slavery as their point of origin in this world. Knowing that they had a rich history and tradition long before slavery that can be linked to their writings via their ancestral DNA may cause them to take their art more serious and draw with a greater sense of purpose. But remember, we have to do our part by enrolling them in art classes or buying the paint and canvases to allow them to participate in the true essence of Hip Hop.

The sacred drum has always played an intricate roll in African societies. It not only represented the external rhythm of the universe, but it also synchronized with the internal rhythm, which is the heartbeat. It speaks a language without using words and it is universally understood by those trained in its secret science. If the village was going to war, they played a certain drum pattern; if a baby was born a certain drum pattern resonated throughout the community. During slavery, slave masters banned the drum because they feared that it was being used to orchestrate uprisings on the plantations, causing many deaths. Over the course of time we were able to integrate the drum back into our culture but it wasn't until the early seventies that a new and innovative way to play the drums using two turntables was invented. The DJ would become the new age drummer, not by design but out of necessity to compensate for the loss of actual drums. The break beats were the instrumental part of a record, usually two seconds or longer that was extended by the use of the second turntable and a mixer. The skill level of the DJ and his or her ability to scratch, cut, and manipulate the record would determine how long the break beat was extended. This is the true definition of Hip Hop, making something out of nothing. The foundation of all music is the beat so the DJ became the most important element in Hip Hop. As Hip Hop evolved, the producer was granted the arduous task of beat maker. The intensity and pace of the drum can and will determine the mood and action of the listener. The listener's heartbeat becomes synchronized with the beats tempo and rhythm until they become one. A lot of Hip Hop drums are angry. This could be a direct result of the environment in which a lot of beat makers are raised in, which is where most of them draw their inspiration. So early Hip Hop was rebellious by nature. When a serene environment is provided; the affects could be the exact opposite. Our youth have the capacity to change the world one (heart) beat at a time.

The break beat had a direct affect on the B-Boys and B-Girls who would articulate the message of the drum with body movements. They would place cardboard on the ground and form a circle around it, building up the energy to a fever pitch in anticipation of the break beat dropping. Once the beat dropped each dancer would be given an equal opportunity to show their skills. No two dance moves would be the same because each dancer had a different interpretation of the language of the drum. The body becomes an instrument or vessel used to convey messages without using sound. Or should I say a very high frequency of sound that the body generates by the different geometrical angles that it forms while in motion. There could be a direct link between the B-Boy and the sacred dancers of ancient antiquity. Our ancestors performed sacred rain dances to ensure that the next season's crops would be fruitful. There were also war dances, ghost dances, sun dances, etc. each serving a specific purpose and was highly spiritual as well. Dancing also has a healing affect. We dance to celebrate life. The therapeutic factors are endless. A fifteen-minute dance recess would probably work wonders for teachers and parents alike. The B-Boy and B-Girl helped the healing begin in the inner cities by simply dancing.

The Emcee is none other than the oracle, the storyteller, the poet, the reverend, the rebel, and philosopher. Even prophets come armed with nothing more than the word. Words are the vessel of thought and when spoken in rhythmic form; they create a very powerful harmonic frequency that becomes the building block for reality itself. The intent of the thought that goes into the word is equally important because thought has a magnetic vibration. If your intention is to change the world for the better using words of love, peace and happiness; chances are you will do just that. First your immediate world will be transformed and then depending on what mechanism is used to amplify your words like microphones, recordings, books, movies, etc. will determine at what rate the world, as a whole will change. Even the Book of Genesis speaks of God using sound vibration to form creation. This is why it is so important to watch your words. But it is even more important guard your thoughts. Another important factor is where you draw your inspiration from to speak. In the Genesis of Hip Hop, the Emcee drew a lot of inspiration from the Civil Rights Movement, soul singers, and activist of that era, but the immediate inspiration was drawn from the environment itself. So when a young lyricist is constantly rapping about drugs, crime, sex and mayhem, it is usually a direct connection to what he or she sees on a daily basis. Without the proper understanding of the magnetism of thought, one can easily use words to create a negative catch 22. If all that our youth rap about is what they see, and what they see is negative; they then create a future based on the same negative energy. And we wonder why the situation in the "Hood" never changes. We need to challenge Emcees and poets to project the future through their positive thoughts and words. Hip Hop is about changing a negative into a positive, and the power of the emcee is a very critical component in changing the world around us.

The history of Hip Hop at its best is a lost generation's subconscious attempt to morph fragments of its glorious past into a new form of expression. While this past may lay dormant or be suppressed from time to time, any number of events or circumstances can unlock or activate the necessary DNA sequences that can bring this reawakening about. In or around the year 1973, the climate was perfect with all of the police brutality, racial climate, unemployment and dismissal of art and music programs in public schools. The reason that I say that this came from the subconscious mind is because most of the early participants of Hip Hop did not intend to bring this change about on a global scale. They were simply addressing the needs of their community by using the tools at their disposal. But that doesn't negate the fact that this small group of inner city teens changed the world with music, art, dance, and the power of the word.

Dr. Martin Luther king Jr. didn't start out to change the world, he too was out to address the immediate needs and concerns of the community he was serving which led to boycotts, strikes, sit ins, etc. The world hasn't been the same since. The history of Hip Hop is the history of our people's struggle in this country for change. Long before gangster rap, commercialism, or the corporate takeover, Hip Hop was the voice of the people by the people. Long before hip-hop was compartmentalized to serve different agendas; it was about "peace, unity, love and havin fun". The legendary founder of Hip Hop culture Afrika Bambaataa who would later state that knowledge was the fifth element of Hip hop coined this phrase. Without the knowledge of our history, without the knowledge of the science of acoustics, without the knowledge of the power of thought, without the knowledge of hieroglyphs, drumming, sacred dancing and the power of words, we do Hip Hop an injustice.

Most of our youth from the inner cities feel like Hip Hop is their way out of the hood, financially. But rarely do they see the importance of using Hip Hop to enhance them spiritually or even culturally for that matter. Hip Hop has yet to fill this void and modern day rap doesn't even acknowledge that there is a void. As long as you're getting paid no matter how degrading or detrimental the lyrics and messages are seems to be the only thing that matters. We have corporate America and the media to thank for that. If parents and teachers can properly teach the history of Hip Hop, then they automatically are teaching about our history as a whole. Hip Hop is just a frequency that our youth are currently tuned into. In order to affectively reach them in any capacity we must align ourselves to that specific frequency. Just as these corporations have Hip Hop commercials to sell their products, we must find a unique way to tune mathematics, science, history, politics, and real economics into the frequency of Hip Hop. Not the other way around since at the current moment, Hip Hop is the frequency with the strongest current. Parents and teachers must ride the wave. The problem is we expend too much energy swimming against the current or going against the grain. What this causes is a standoff between figures of authority (parents, teachers) and "rebellious" youth. If you can't beat them, join them but join them with the understanding that we are guides. And no matter how much they may deny it; they are truly looking for guidance. So find the diamonds in the ruff within Hip Hop. Today's rap is not a true reflection of Hip Hop as a whole, but we can still use it to gage the current temperament of our youth, and then aggressively match it with the energy and spirit of real Hip Hop.

CHAPTER 4

FROM HIP HOP TO RAP

Yes, there is a difference. Parents and teachers, if you want to impress your students and children, *know* the difference. As the last chapter explained, Hip Hop is culturally based. It is spiritual in nature. It deals with all of the elements of art in unison, creating a new synergistic art form that we call Hip Hop. Just as earth, air, fire, and water come together to create all that we see in this world, Hip Hop is also created of these same elements...well, sort of.

The characteristics of the four elements of Hip Hop are very similar. The graffiti writer (hieroglyph) is earth-based since there has to be an early substance in which the art is displayed. The DJ (ancient drummer) is air-based since sound uses air to travel. The B-Boy/Girl (sacred dancers) is water-based since the body is composed of over 70% water. And the Emcee (oracle) is fire-based since the word when spoken with intensity and truth has the capability to burn through any illusion. This is where Emcees get the term "spittin fire". When all of the elements of Hip Hop come together they are alchemical in nature. Alchemy is the science of transforming lead to gold or transforming man into God.

Hip Hop transformed a people from the lowest of the low, to highest of the high, socially, economically, politically, even spiritually. Hip Hop has transformed the world. It is the capstone of all other music genres. It is the only genre that uses all of the other genres of music that came before it. Embedded within Hip Hop are our ancient past, our recent struggles, and our future plight for freedom, justice, and equality. When the principles of Hip Hop are applied correctly, they have the ability to crack the code of what is plaguing our youth today. It is important to note that Hip Hop is love based. Before you can profit from your skills you had to be willing to participate and harness your skills for the love of the culture first and foremost. Hip Hop is based in creativity. It prides itself on being original. Each artist took pride in studying the craft to find out what was missing, and then filling that void. Sounding like someone else or imitating someone else's style was a violation of Hip Hop law. Hip Hop is intelligent. The more intelligence displayed within the art form, the greater the praise one received. Hip Hop is a tool used to entertain, educate, heal, and inspire. Hip Hop is about balance. Each of the elements is equally important and is recognized as an intricate part to the culture. Now, let's talk about…Rap.

Rap is the polar opposite of Hip Hop. It is a watered down version reserved for those with a lesser skill base. Rap has no principles, codes of ethics, or laws by which it is governed. Anything and everything goes. Rap is palatable Hip Hop for those who do not, nor truly care to understand the culture itself. Rap omits the B-Boy, graph writer, even the DJ in some cases. It focuses primarily on easy to recite lyrics usually of a degrading nature and is not intended to raise the vibration of the people. Rap is not intended to enlighten, inspire, or bring awareness to any cause that may be troubling the community. It is party music. And party music of the lowest level. It is stripper music. It is drug-selling music. It is violent music, and corporations love it!

Corporations created the Rap music industry, why? Because it was much easier for them to digest. Hip Hop in its truest form is too advanced for corporations to understand or appreciate. The rhyme patterns and metaphors were too complex to grasp. The dance moves were too intricate and untraditional. The signs, symbols and archetypes of the graffiti writers were too elaborate to the uninitiated. The DJs ability to manipulate the sound of a record and alter its essence by moving it back and forth in rhythmic patterns made no sense to a suit on Wall Street. Add to the mix the Pro-Black militant songs that were galvanizing the people, and it's easy to see that this made White America nervous. So in order to cash in on this new phenomenon drastic changes needed to be made in order to sell it to the general public. It needed to be dumbed down. The lyrics needed to be simplified with catchy hooks that were easy to sing along to. It needed to be safe and funny and harmless to the establishment.

To complete this transition, many Hip Hop artists were faded out and record labels began to sign rappers in their place. By the mid 1990's the transition was complete. With the exception of a few die-hard Hip Hop artists who were able to stand the test of time, Rap music was birthed with the focus geared toward partying, selling drugs, violence, degrading women, and selling products. Rappers were detached from anything remotely close to Hip Hop. Gone were the days when artist stood up and used their voices for noble causes. Fame and money became the driving force of Rap music. It is widely known in the movie industry that sex and violence sells. But never before has an opportunity to use music for the same purpose been explored and exploited until Rap was born. Once co-opted, corporations could use rap to promote any agenda that they saw fit. Rap artist were paid handsomely to promote products that are detrimental to our health like alcohol, soda, and fast food. Rap became cross-promotional; so Rap artist found themselves in movies, fashion shows, and television sitcoms. Even promoting the selling of drugs and the use of firearms allowed the prison industry to thrive as prisons began to fill up with wanna be rappers and gangsters leading the way. Hip Hop is esoteric in nature. It is for a chosen few who understand the power of art and the potential that it has if properly applied. It represents the spiritual realm or higher degrees of music.

Rap is exoteric in nature. It is for everyone. Anyone can rap with no prior training or connection to Hip Hop whatsoever. Rap is what is given to the masses, and we all know that old saying "the masses are Asses." It represents the material or lower realms of music. It is not just rap music that is lowering the vibration of the planet. Music, movies and the media collectively are casting a web over the planet that is affecting the thinking and actions of the populace. All three of these mediums are interchangeable now. So the culture of Hip Hop is what parents and teachers should embrace, it's Rap music that is causing most of the problems. But since Hip Hop gave birth to Rap, it too has to except some of the blame for the path that it has taken. Rap has become the Black Sheep of the family, but at the end of the day, it is still family. As the saying goes "never throw the baby out with the bath water," we have to reunite Rap back with its true family in hopes that it can have a positive affect on generations to come.

CHAPTER 5

URBAN CULTURE

N ow that we have a clear distinction between Hip Hop and rap let's look at the word culture as it pertains to Hip Hop, Rap, and the urban environment that produced both. The word culture as it relates to Hip Hop is worth discussing because most people do not believe that it is a culture. Since Hip Hop gave birth to Rap, which then gave birth to urban culture, we will use Hip Hop as the reference point. Then we will decipher some of the sub-cultures that encompass urban Culture as a whole.

First, let's examine the term and definition of the word and then we can apply the meaning to Hip Hop to see where it leads us. According to the American Heritage Dictionary, culture means the totality of socially transmitted behavior patterns, arts, beliefs, institutions, and all other products of human work and thought. It goes on to state; culture is the intellectual and artistic activity and the works produced by it. It also means to cultivate. Hip Hop has contributed immensely to the social behavior patterns of youth all over the world. It has shaped the minds of the last two generations to be exact. Show me a child that has not been directly or indirectly influenced by Hip Hop and I will show you a child that has been living in a vacuum. The importance of art as it relates to culture has already been covered extensively, so let's move on to beliefs. Most cultures have a belief system that has already been in place since its inception, a belief system that holds the core values of the culture and is collectively agreed upon by its followers. Not Hip Hop. Hip Hop is fluid. It's swift and changeable. So it has no set belief system and won't allow itself to be boxed in or contained in ways that traditional cultures have in the past. It is the crystalized point of *all* belief systems, meaning, if it can be qualified through art, thought, intellectually or through the actions of ones ways; then Hip Hop will embrace it and believe in its power.

Everything is everything in Hip Hop. Its belief system is based on its ability to find the artistic approach to reveal and express truth within all cultures. If your art moves the people and has a profound impact on their way of life, then a "Hip Hop" belief system is established. When we speak about belief in general, most people just focus on the religious aspect of it, or the laws by which the culture is governed, but anything that you give your core (center) to, is a part of that overall belief system. Now lets look at institution as it concerns culture. Institution is the practice, relationship, or organization within a society. It is also someone or something firmly associated with a place or thing. Each movement in Hip Hop is an institution within itself. The Hip Hop group Public Enemy is an institution. Jay Z's Roc Nation is an institution. Just as Rick Ross's Maybach Music is an institution as well. Each has their core members; they have their followers that believe in their *way of life*, which is also the meaning of culture. Their works have had a great impact on the lives of so many, especially the youth, and will most likely change the course of history. But unlike the institution of marriage or baseball, Hip Hop will define and redefine itself every generation. Hip Hop is not going anywhere, so parents and teachers take note and study it well. Culture also means to cultivate, which means to grow. Growth brings growing pains and Hip Hop has had its ups and downs along the way, but it has grown nonetheless.

The Pioneers of Hip Hop are now grandmothers and grandfathers so we now have an eldership of the culture that has retained the true history of the origins of the culture. The seeds of the culture are deeply planted now and if the original principles are preserved, Hip Hop will continue to grow. Hip Hop has grown from a street art form that had no relevance, to now being taught as a course study in most of our institutions of higher learning. The economic base that it has generated is unparalleled in American History and abroad. Billions of dollars can be directly attributed to Hip Hop's presence. This means the culture can financially sustain itself. Just look at the economy before Hip Hop was introduced into the lexicon of corporate America and look at it now…. any question? For the first time in American history, the political force of Hip Hop was felt during the 2008 presidential election as president Barack Obama won in a landslide. Many Hip Hop and Rap artist came out in support of Obama, which led to the largest turn out of young people at the polls that America has ever seen. There is even a Hip Hop Action Network that focuses on the political voices of a younger generation. The last frontier of a culture is usually the higher sciences, philosophies, or spiritual teachings. Thanks to the spiritual insight of Afrika Bambaataa, KRS ONE, the likes of myself, and many more, we are beginning to lay the foundation of the higher principles of our culture for generations to come. Can you imagine what the next 40 years will add to the culture?

So lets sum up culture as it relates to Hip Hop. It has its own art form, language, laws (stop snitchin), political movements, and even its own religion, which is that all religions are welcomed. Hip Hop as a curriculum will soon be mandatory in schools from elementary to college. The older hip-hop becomes, the more it has the opportunity and capacity to branch off from its roots and affect all aspects of our daily life. Just turn on the television or open a newspaper, magazine, or turn on the radio to understand this phenomenon called Hip Hop. Hip Hop has generated its own economy. There are many artists within the Hip Hop community that have no formal education but are millionaires. Soon Hip Hop will have its first billionaire that has risen from the ranks of artists, to the height of C.E.O. These are the components that make up a culture even if not in the traditional sense. Most cultures have demographic, religious, racial, or ethnic boundaries. Hip Hop breaks all of those rules. So to understand it, you must be willing to shed tradition. This may cause a problem for parents who are trying to instill the value of culture into their children but the children do not see the need for it to be successful. Culture is a way of life, and this way of life may not resonate with those stuck in a culture void. Many cultural traditions are past down from generation to generation without a single question being asked regarding its validity. Hip Hop is your child's way of asking questions. Just as you would show respect to someone else's culture, even if you do not fully understand it; Hip Hop must be given the same respect. And since Hip Hop is swift and changeable, you may find it easy to incorporate into your already existing way of life. To make it simple, communication with you children or students on a level that shows respect for what they like and think, and doing it in a language that they can understand is participating in Hip Hop culture.

CHAPTER 6

THE SUB-CULTURE

E very culture over the course of time develops a sub culture. One that resembles the culture but has carved out niches that suits a portion of the original followers who are dissatisfied or are rebelling against the culture itself. Hip Hop is no different. Rap is a part of the sub culture, but it is a small part. In this chapter I will deal with the many faces of urban culture. These elements are critical for those attempting to understand the youth of today. Most youth are involved with some or all of these elements in one capacity or another. The components of urban life are unique in the sense that what is looked down upon in other communities are a part of the survival tactics or way of life in urban communities. But I need to preface what I am about to say with the understanding that the challenges that our children are facing are like nothing we have ever seen in our lifetime. If you are over 40 years old then you know exactly what I am talking about. We didn't have the Internet to deal with which opened windows to worlds of violence, sex, and other inappropriate things that most children were not ready to experience. We didn't have anything called social media to exploit us or apply levels of peer pressure on us to be someone or something that we were not. We didn't have smart phones to distract us or diminish our true social skills, which can only be accomplished with real human-to-human interaction. We didn't have music the glorified violence, sex, and drug selling or record labels that endorsed such behavior just to make a profit. We didn't have the many sexual orientations, or sexual classifications that this generation is accustomed to. We didn't have our favorite artist or athletes promoting destructive products for us to consume everyday.

The obesity, drug, and incarceration rate have increased tenfold since corporate America began cutting checks for these services. We didn't have dangerous prescription drugs being administered to children just because they were a little hyperactive or had so called behavioral problems. The side affects are usually worse than the drugs prescribed. We didn't have fast food as our only source of nutrition. We had home-cooked meals and we drank water. As a result the chemical warfare that is being launched against this generation didn't exist. We didn't have violent video games that launched us into virtual realities that seemed so real that we began to act out and commit these crimes in real life. We never had to deal with the media or get bombarded with propaganda, which shaped and controlled our thought process. Mind control is real. We didn't have to deal with gang bangers that forced you to join their clique or suffer dire consequences. We didn't glorify going to prison as a rights of passage or some kind of badge of honor. Meanwhile, the children who strive to better themselves by going to college are barely recognized or those who underachieved despise them. We didn't have to deal with a generation that is so detached from its culture and history that they don't even know who Harriet Tubman, George Washington Carver, Malcolm X, or Thurgood Marshall is, just to name a few.

So before we pass judgment, we need to understand that the world that they have inherited in much different. And it's still changing as we speak. The deck has been stacked against them in ways that make it seem impossible for this generation to win. So as a result of this, it should be easy for us to see that culture as a whole is trending downward. With that being said it's still imperative that we address the many sub cultures that have emerged as a result of the climate that has been set by America so that we can begin the process of rebuilding a better future for our youth...

CHAPTER 7

THE DRUG GAME

Selling drugs in urban communities is as American as apple pie. In fact, drug selling in urban communities is an institution. Without getting too deep into the "conspiracy" theory about who put the drugs there in the first place, drugs are the main staple by which the economy in the hood thrives and suffers at the same time. It is the main impediment by which some people make it out of the hood and some people are trapped forever. It is the driving force by which some are motivated to overcome and defeat the system, and those who never rise above the traps, and get caught up and processed *into* the system. And ultimately it is the main reason in which some people in the hood live to be old, or die very young. This is the harsh reality of it. Selling drugs is not even looked upon as a crime in most urban neighborhoods; it's a way of life. And if this is the path that you choose, unless you are a minor, you fully understand the consequences that come with it. Death or prison time is well worth the risk, but being poor and doing nothing about it is not. For young people growing up in the hood, seeing a drug dealer is like seeing the mailman, both provide a service that is needed.

The drug dealer/drug user relationship is an interesting dynamic to say the least. They both live in the same neighborhood and interact with the same people. Their level of education is generally the same. Their families know each other. The economics is the only thing that separates them, barely. A drug dealer is one bust away from being in the same boat as a drug user. Most of them are not even smart enough to set aside bail money for the inevitable. The government funds both. The government has to be complicit in some shape, form, or fashion for high levels of drugs to make it to the hood. We don't own any poppy seed fields, plants to manufacture drugs or the capabilities to distribute drugs throughout this country.

Let's not be naive. The government also funds the user every month with food stamps, public assistance, and other stipends that are supposed to be used to really help and support those families in need but are instead used to purchase drugs and support drug habits. Let's not be naive about this aspect either. This is not to suggest that all families on public assistance are drug abusers and do not benefit from the help of government subsidies. But on the 1st and the 15th of every month, there is so much money changing hands and so many transactions taking place that the hood looks like the stock exchange down on Wall Street. This energy is only generated when government funds are being issued which is usually on or around these dates. Every Hustlers handbook has these dates circled. Their lifestyle depends on it. But what's interesting is that the higher the drug dealer moves up the economic ladder, the lower he sinks the economics and moral of his own community. The more his material possessions rise, the more dead bodies fall. The more his dreams are fulfilled, the more dreams he shatters. And yet he is looked upon as a hero when he comes and hands out turkeys on Thanksgiving. He is respected by his peers, adored by the ladies, and feared by his foes. Drugs are the life force and death force of urban America.

Back in the 70's and 80's B.C. (before Crack), the street was filled with a different type of drug dealer, one who had street codes and ethics, if there is such a thing. They didn't sell to children. They would not let children sell drugs for them. They literally fed and housed people in need. They wouldn't put innocent people in harms way by violently spraying bullets into a crowd. They went to church on Sundays and tithed very handsomely. They wouldn't kill innocent family members as retribution for another hustler's actions. They encouraged young people to get an education and stay away from the streets. If you did choose to hustle the best street hustlers around properly trained you in the ways of the streets and how to conduct business. And most importantly, they were not proud of what they did and would never brag or promote such a lifestyle. Flash to the modern day drug dealer and this scenario is reversed. They sell to anybody that has the money, including children, pregnant women, elderly, etc. They use children to sell drugs and be lookouts. They will shoot into a crowd with no regards for innocent life. They will come to your home and kill your babies for a debt that hasn't been paid. They glorify the lifestyle. Some rub elbows with the elite entertainers and athletes. Some even become rappers themselves and boast about all of the drugs they sell. And this is perfectly accepted in urban America.

Now the next generation of hustlers who were birthed in the crack era, who weren't properly trained in the science of drug dealing (yes I said science) is on a different mission. "Rappers" who endorse this life heavily influence them. They even glorify the television specials that profile some of the biggest drug dealers that America has ever seen. Some even take on the names and monikers of their favorite dealers. They are looking to get rich and famous. Even the "rappers" who don't really live that lifestyle and have never sold drugs a day in their lives continue to profit from this miscarriage of justice. And we wanna know what's wrong with our youth, and why they don't go to school, or have respect for their elders? Money is king. With very few resources in the hood, the ends will justify the means. But the economic landscape continues to suffer because these same individuals who profit from selling drugs literally and metaphorically do not have the financial wit and foresight to invest their money into legitimate businesses with the exception of the rap game, which we will discuss later. So there is no silver lining besides a few cars, watches, and homes, which will all be confiscated as soon as the feds roll up. What if we broke the cycle by having every drug dealer sponsor a kid to college? How crazy would that be? Let's be honest. Everybody in the hood doesn't have the mental capacity to academically thrive in a college setting. Most hustlers know that for them this is the end of the road. But there are many who have a legit chance but lack the necessary funds to achieve their goals. If this was done properly, then the term "Stop Snitchin" would take on a whole new meaning because the hood would have a vested interest in the profits being made from selling drugs. And this would have to be done with no strings attached. The college student would not be indebted to the hustler. However, when the drug dealer is finally arrested (if not killed first) and has to spend time in prison reflecting on the mistakes he or she has made, and is looking for a second chance at life, maybe one of these students who benefited from this program will be the one to lend a helping hand. It will be that same student who understands that the drug dealer had potential to be much more in life but circumstances led to bad choices. How crazy would that be? Now what was once a negative cycle has potential to be an upward trending cycle, or a break-even cycle at worse.

I told you in the beginning of this book that we need to explore unconventional methods to our problems, so before you lynch me, please consider that this business model is not too far off from the way the mafia succeeded. The one difference, and I admit that it is a big one; The Mafia didn't sell drugs to their own people. But they did use the proceeds to establish legitimate businesses like restaurants, construction businesses, and other companies. Pay very close attention to the marijuana industry. The government has adopted this very concept and it has been successful thus far. We are in crises mode as a people so our survival is at stake. The complexity of the situation is how do you kill and save your community at the same time? If we are talking about our survival, maybe the ends do justify the means.

CHAPTER 8

TO TWERK OR NOT TO TWERK?

THAT IS THE QUESTION!

Chuck D from the legendary Hip Hop group Public Enemy stated, "Attention is the new currency." If this is the case, then the Internet has provided new revenue streams for young women with high quality figures and low self-esteem. Young women showing off their bodies and dancing in a suggestive manner called twerking has taken the country by storm. Normally this type of adult entertainment would be reserved for those who were at a nightclub and everyone there would be of age. But the Internet has opened up a whole new vortex by which access to what used to be private and sacred is available to anyone and everyone. As a result, young women seeking attention are more willing to expose themselves in a sexual manner because the number of hits she receives can literally quantify the results. Each hit is like a charge of energy, a vote of confidence. So can you imagine what 800,000 hits does to the psyche of a young women who doesn't have a father at home to teach her about her value beyond her physical appearance?

A lot of young women have been relegated to using their physical attributes to gain favor with men, why? Could it be that every song that they hear on the radio is making some kind of sexual reference? Or could it be that every female artist that they listen to and watch is half dressed and using their bodies to sell records and gain popularity? Miley Cyrus brought national attention to the culture of twerking during the 2013 MTV awards. Her core audience is young females who grew with her from her Hanna Montana days. What most people didn't realize is that Miley Cyrus was performing a ritual to kill off Hannah Montana, and give birth to the new, all grownup young woman ready to explore life's challenges, including sex. The ripple effect of such actions is that many young girls whose sexual energy is not ready to be activated are thrust into a world of sexual chaos and confusion. Most people may view this as harmless since there is just visual stimulation involved, but visual stimulation can become a gateway for physical contact. Twerking is a part of the culture. In fact, it has always been a part of the culture of Black people, we just didn't call it twerking. Some say the origin of the dance is from New Orleans, which was called bounce music. Others say Miami started the craze. It may actually go all the way back to West Africa with a dance called Mapouka which is a very suggestive dance that was performed ceremoniously, and I'm pretty sure the name will change again in the near future. But what will not change are young women showing off their bodies in a sexual manner for attention. We live in a visual dimension now. This is why sites like YouTube and Worldstar Hip Hop are so popular.

For this generation if you do not have an existence in the virtual world, you do not exist, period. Twerking has provided an existence for those young women who would otherwise be anonymous. They matter, even if it's just as a part of somebody's fantasy. Yet fantasy is the new reality. I will say it again…fantasy is the new reality. So a million hits is like a million minds banning together to form an alternate universe that allows ones fantasies to become real, even if just temporarily. Attention is a powerful energy source. It should not be taken lightly. In fact, the greatest gift that any parent can give their child is time. So when we give the proper time and attention to our children they have a lesser need to receive it in the virtual world.

CHAPTER 9

THE CULTURE OF STRIPPING

How do you tell a young woman who can make ten thousand dollars a night stripping that she should stop, go to school, acquire a degree, and if she is lucky she could earn fifty thousand dollars a year? How do you tell a young woman who has watched her mother struggle her entire life to pay bills on dead-end jobs just to keep food on the table, that making money hand over foot is the wrong thing to do? America has always been a capitalist society but this new generation has taken this concept to new heights...or should I say new lows. Anything that makes money is acceptable, and I mean anything. There are no moral boundaries by which they abide by. Selling sex, stripping, drugs, and petty crimes are all great sources of tax-free income. In the hood, your motivations are never questioned or have to be rationalized when you are making money by these means. It's the hoods way of beating the system. The culture of stripping is very lucrative. Young women used to strip as a means to pay tuition for college but now strippers are doing so well financially that college is no longer in their plans. They are stripping as a way of life. Stripping has become so much a part of the culture that in some cities you have to pay taxes on the proceeds made. The rap industry is largely responsible for taking what was considered as underground business and popularizing it to the point where even mainstream America recognizes it as a legitimate business or at least a legit form of entertainment. When you also consider the web sites and Rap blogs that profile these strippers on a daily basis, it's easy to see how a stripper can become a celebrity in her own right. Rappers, "Ballers" and athletes have elevated the status of the most common stripper from the lowest of the low, to the highest plateau in entertainment. This is done mainly through song, video, even relationships. Some rappers and high profile athletes even marry strippers.

Just ten years ago, marrying a stripper was considered to be taboo. Most of us are looking at an immoral world through a moral lens trying to make sense of it all. Young people are more influenced by athletes and celebrities than their own parents. So they struggle upholding the moral values that have been instilled in them at home when their favorite rapper or athlete is promoting the very opposite behavior. Young women see high profile athletes spending astronomical amounts of money to admire the physical attribute of strippers, so why should they attempt to develop their mental or spiritual prowess? Yes, this culture has reduced the female energy to nothing more than a physical specimen. However, in their eyes they are being "rewarded" handsomely for it. Young men see their favorite Rapper or celebrity literally throwing money on beautiful young women so often that they begin to associate women with being nothing more than the objects of their physical affections. When we also consider that most of these young men grew up without a father or father figure to teach them about the true value of women, then we should not be surprised that they will only use women, especially strippers for their sexual exploits. It gets deeper. Why would a young man want a "regular" woman who goes to school or works a 9 to 5 job, who has certain principles and values that won't allow herself to be exploited? Why would he want a young woman who is not popular, one that is not lusted for by many men, or one whose sexual reputation is not that of legend? Better yet, why would any young woman want to be considered "regular" when most of the men she meets are looking past her to get at the stripper type women? Why would she attempt to develop a mental or spiritual bond with a man that could lead to some strange phenomenon called "love" when the only thing he has been trained to do is admire her body. Yes we live in "Bizarro" World where up is down and left is right.

We live in a world where frequenting strip clubs is a sign of success now. What was once done in the dark and considered lowly is now done under the bright lights and is considered flying high. Unlike twerking, which only generates virtual currency by way of attention, stripping pays big bucks. Scholarship money is wasted at high-end strip clubs on a regular basis. Enough money to open up small businesses is spent at the bar alone! So the value of money from an economic standpoint is taken for granted. We don't see the need to invest our money wisely, easy come, easy go has always been the hood motto. So the path for a lot of young women growing up in the hood these days may bypass the course of going to college, finding a decent young man to settle down with and raise a family. That's old paradigm. Her vision may include twerking, with hopes of making it to an elite club to strip for high-end ballers, hustlers, Rappers and athletes. If "money" is the end all and be all, can you blame her? We have to place a higher value on life and salute those women who still hold certain aspects of life true and dear. We have to shine the light on those young women who are spiritually in tune with self who understand their true value as Queens of the universe. We as men have to show by our actions that we need more than just physical stimulation to help us achieve our goals in life as well. We as men have to demonstrate that we love, honor and respect our women or we will perish as a community. But as long as money is God, then our young women and men will continue to praise it. They will continue to worship all that it brings. Until that day comes when we understand our true self worth, stripping will always be an intricate part of our cultureculture. men will continue to praise it. They will continue to worship all that it brings. Until that day comes when we understand our true self worth, stripping will always be an intricate part of our culture.

CHAPTER 10

SELLING SEX / "BOOTY" CLUBS / PIMP GAME

The darkest side of the culture is the straight sex game. Where twerking may be visual and stripping may be seen as fantasy on some levels, there is only one stage left, that's physical sex. Now before we move any further, we know and understand that prostitution is one of the oldest professions in the world, so I will not spend a lot of time giving a history lesson or doing a psychoanalysis on why young women would choose to go this route. I only want to examine it from a cultural viewpoint. This is just another part of the panoramic view of the culture that we have embarked upon so that we can get a better understanding of what life is like in urban America. Selling sex is an essential part of it. Women have detached themselves emotionally to the point where selling their bodies is just another viable source of income and nothing more. It's a job, and it's a job that over the course of time has received less scrutiny than in the past. Times are changing all around us, and culture has morphed into what we do, see, and act upon everyday that provides joy, money, or value to our lives. So women and men alike have rationalized this behavior as normal hood protocol for making money, and the sex game has provided many avenues in which this is done.

First, let's deal with the booty clubs. They began to pop up when it became a little more dangerous for young ladies to be on the streets. Not only were they being harassed by the police for illegal activities, a lot of dangerous characters began to threaten their well-being, rob them, or assault them. So these small incognito type clubs began to open with multiple rooms, poles, and bars to accommodate patrons. The atmosphere is usually very dark and gloomy and most people who frequent these spots are trying to be as anonymous as possible. These spots don't require a pimp so to speak but there are usually bodyguards there to ensure the safety of the ladies. The workers usually "tip in" which mean they pay a small fee upon entry into the club and whatever proceeds that make is theirs. They set their own prices for their services. The club itself usually works on a membership basis via email or Facebook using code words, phrases, etc. The customers also have to pay a fee to enter the spot. There are multiple types of booty clubs, some that serve the wealthy and some that serve the working class. The ones that tend to the wealthy are usually very private and exclusive. You may even have to sign a confidentiality agreement. They are usually packed with athletes, hustlers, rappers, and other famous to do people. The working class booty clubs are a little more assessable. But the ultimate goal of both spots is the same: sex.

For the women who work theses spots it's usually long hours, physically exhausting and degrading work in some cases, but the money is good. The women who work the exclusive spots obviously receive a few more perks, like bigger tips, champagne, and if she is lucky, a call back to work one-on-one with a famous customer. For the women who work the hood, it's a much different economic base in which prices are negotiated, haggled, and there are rarely any perks. These places operate like a meat market. Women walk by scantily dressed and if you like what you see, you buy. Now there are still many women who work the streets, and a pimp is usually involved in some capacity. The process by which a pimp convinces a woman to sell her body and then give him the money requires deep, deep analysis in which time will not allow for me to go too in-depth. But the basic principle of that relationship is still economics. He is empowered by the services that she provides. Morally this is twisted, but culturally accepted. The true power lies with the women working because without her there is no him. But pimps have done a masterful job working on the esteem of a lot of weak women. As a result, they live a lavish life and the women continue to decay, mentally, physically, and spiritually. And when she can no longer provide economic stability, she is discarded like a piece of trash. The pimp constantly recruits so that his cash flow never ceases. Let's go even deeper. There are many levels of the pimp game. Most don't even involve women selling their bodies. A pimp is anybody that can convince people to follow them or their cause for the sake of making money, usually for the pimp only. Politicians can be pimps, so are some pastors, Gurus, rappers, etc. In the hood, any means by which you are making a living is considered an honest living. I never stated that evaluating the culture would lead to a moral road map that we could follow to help guide us to a place where this all made sense. Truth be told, the answers we are looking for lie between the moral and immoral lines of existence, and is truly a matter of perception. Let us continue…

CHAPTER 11

THE SNEAKER GAME

U rban culture has many facets to it and sneakers are a big part of its foundation. When we see young people spending the night outside of a sneaker store waiting to purchase the latest pair of Air Jordan's we automatically call them insane. And if we are just looking at it from a mundane level we are absolutely correct. But beyond the mundane lies an artistic expression that only resonates with this generation. Beyond the mundane lies a cultural statement that is made with every fresh pair of kicks worn and the adoration one receives from friends, even envious peers. Beyond the mundane is the elite status bestowed upon one who rocks an original pair of kicks in the hood, and that's worth spending a couple of cold nights on a city sidewalk with hundreds of others in anticipation of a new release. Symbolically speaking, our feet represent our ability to move forward. They represent our ability to step into the unknown. Our feet are our foundation in which everything else stands upon. Our feet are also our direct connection with the earth. The old saying "The journey of a thousand miles begins with the first step" is a metaphor for conquering fear, making progress, and overcoming life's obstacles. But when you grow up in the hood, that journey seems like a million miles. So a fresh pair of sneakers means that they are going places, even if it's just metaphorically speaking. Every new pair of kicks means a renewed commitment to their struggle for survival. Every new pair of kicks is like a fresh start on life which knocked them down the day before. When one can't afford a new pair of sneakers, it says that his or her journey is stagnant. It represents more than just the economics of that person; it represents their state of mind. I know that sounds like a far stretch in the minds of most adults, but to understand this concept you have to remove the veil of adulthood and see things through the eyes of an inner city child. Status is everything, and this phenomenon is not just regulated to children or young adults. Grown men are heavily vested in the sneaker game as well.

This is where the problem truly lies. Dr. Francis Cress Welsing in her book, "The Isis Papers" gave a masterful breakdown of the psychological affects of wearing sneakers and how it keeps us in perpetual motion to nowhere. The true purpose of a pair of sneakers is to participate in a game of some sort or sporting event. When we constantly wear sneakers it keeps us in game mode and in a recreational state of being. In other words, we never grow up. Even the term "Player" which is often used in the hood to mean a ladies man or hustler can be tied back to wearing sneakers. If life is a game, then we are the ones being played by our inability to grow up and face the challenges that it presents in a manner that says we are men, not boys. Dr. Francis Cress Welsing was spot on. How do we expect society as a whole to respect us when a man's sneaker collection is far greater than his book collection? How can we be taken seriously when we will kill someone over a sneaker that cost $12 to make? Who truly places the value on these sneakers?

1985 was the year that truly changed everything regarding this sneaker revolution. Nike released its first pair of Air Jordan's and the world as we knew it would never be the same. The multi-colored sneaker was actually banned from the N.B.A. but was a major hit with the youth of that era. Legendary filmmaker, Spike Lee is the one that gave birth to the iconography that is Michael Jordan. His commercials were funny, scientific, and presented in short-film mode. The black and white film gave his commercials more of an artistic feel to them. Michael Jordan's aerial dynamics and superb agility coupled with Spike Lee's vision created the mythological figure and the footwear of the Gods. There's an old African proverb that says, "I am because we are" so Michaels ascension to the top of the world was a collective effort, and wearing his sneakers was a way to participate in his journey. Every time he reached a new level, a new sneaker was released to commemorate that success. So it's much deeper than a $12 shoe being sold for $250. The shoe is charged with the spirit of Michael Jordan. The iconic logo of Michael leaping over all obstacles is symbolic of every young mans dreams growing up in the hood.

We all want to rise above life's challenges and slay our adversaries. There are those who collect watches, cars, diamonds, and art. But when someone collects sneakers they are looked down upon. Art is art. And to this generation sneakers have an artistic value to them. Some even sell for thousands of dollars at sneaker conventions, so whether we agree with it or not, this portion of the culture will continue to thrive. Michael Jordan hasn't played in over ten years but his sneaker continues to fly off the shelves as men young and old continue to place artistic value in them. Economically speaking we continue to suffer from "Hood" ignorance as to where and when to spend our dollars. There is still a large portion of the community that blame Michael Jordan for the destruction and mayhem that takes place regarding his sneakers, and rightfully so. Not once has Michael stepped forward to say please stop the violence; your life is far more valuable than a pair of sneakers. Nike understands that this is about art, and how does art keep its value? It keeps its value with exclusivity, scarcity, and high price points. So artistically speaking, this is in line with everything else that is considered valuable art.

For most of us adults, it's hard to grasp the concept of a sneaker having any true value. But the sneaker represents so much more to a poverty stricken culture. I believe that every male should own a pair of shoes. You automatically take on a different mindset when wearing hard bottom shoes in particular. One doesn't have time for games when in a nice pair of shoes. Maybe we can convince the youth to see the cultural value within themselves by simply switching from a sneaker to a shoe, even if just for a brief moment or so.

CHAPTER 12

THE CULTURE OF SPORTS

"Either you slinging crack rock, or you gotta wicked jump shot."
-Notorious B.I.G.

This was a very profound statement made by the Notorious B.I.G. because it illustrates that the options are few and far in between when you grow up in urban America, and there is a thin line between the right side of the law and the wrong side, and neither is looked upon as negative as long as the ends justify the means. Each is looked upon as a particular skill set used as a tool for survival. Navigating through the streets avoiding the police with deceptive tactics is no different than dribbling through two defenders and throwing a no look pass to a teammate. It all depends on what your "game" is. It's a matter of basic mathematics used by a hustler. He has to master the science of supply and demand, or geometry by a ball player using a round ball aimed at a cylinder, sometimes from behind an arc with a square background played on a rectangle court. Basketball is the main sport played in urban America. This is mainly due to the concrete terrain inhabited by urban dwellers. Basketball is a rite of passage. It is a prerequisite for most males to learn the science of basketball at an early age. It is the first place where you have to learn to grow up and fast. The basketball court is tough, aggressive, competitive, and quickly separates the boys from the men. It is the first place where a lot of young men who don't have fathers at home will meet their elder mentors who will show them no mercy when in between the lines.

Idle time is a vice, so if nothing else, playing basketball keeps most young men preoccupied with something other than selling drugs or committing petty crimes. The street game is a lot different than organized ball. There are no set rules in the street so you have to develop the mental toughness and capacity to deal with anything and everything, no blood, no foul. It prepares you for life in the hood where things aren't always fair. The basketball court is the ultimate platform where ones physical skills are put on display for the entire hood to see, admire, and awe over. Dancing is a way of speaking without using words. The greater the dancer, the higher the frequencies reached, then the more profound the affect it will have on those watching. Well, playing a sport that requires one to move in a designed or premeditated manner is the same thing. It is a sacred dance that is choreographed and played on a court or ball field. So ones ability to dribble, cut, maneuver, spin, and fly can only truly be appreciated by those who understand the language being spoken. Sure, everyone can speak the general dialect of the game, but only a chosen few can speak the advanced language of basketball, and they are revered as Gods. You can learn a lot about a person by the way that they play sports. It will tell you if they have vision, if they are a team player, if they are willing to sacrifice, is there commitment, and if they can be counted on. Are these not the same attributes that corporate America requires for employment? So what one lacks in academics or a "corporate" mindset is easily expressed through sports. The ironic thing about it is that the same corporations that shunned a player from the hood earlier because of his lack of corporate etiquette will be breathing down their necks once they emerge from high school and the college ranks as potential superstars who can sell products. Yet that is a long, hard, and arduous process to even get to a point where ones talent can take them far beyond the hood.

It all begins with the love of the game and as a recreational outlet that quickly turns into a way of life for most youth who begin to see this as their meal ticket out of poverty, and who can blame them when every time they turn on the television athletes are celebrated like rock stars. Athletes who look just like them or come from the same background as them are driving nice cars and live in extremely extravagant homes. For them, the blueprint has already been laid out, stay way from drugs, attend just enough classes to fulfill the necessary requirements to pass, and harness their skill set. Where academics may come hard, playing the game comes easy. The basketball court, and the football field to a lesser extent is where the first great separation begins. Those with extraordinary skills are set apart for the mediocre ballers, who then have to find another outlet, which is usually selling drugs or rapping, (which we will get to in a moment). Academics are usually the fourth outlet. Or in the case of a skilled athlete, it is just a means by which they can advance their playing career beyond the hood and nothing more. Back in the days, they didn't even have to do that. Exceptional Athletes were given passing grades even if they could not read or write because it benefited the school to have an opportunity to win games and gain some notoriety at the same time. This is not to suggest that academics are not important or that there are not many young brothers and sisters who take full advantage of the educational system to blossom in other fields like science, medicine, law, etc. I am simply stating that the majority of young people from the hood are entrenched in survival mode from such an early age that education rarely moves to the forefront. So culturally speaking, sports are a tool that is used to reach the ultimate goal which is to "make it" in the world. In the hood, when one makes it, we all make it. So athletes are carrying the entire urban community on their shoulders. It was no different than when Jackie Robinson was brought up to play professionally for the Dodgers in 1955, or Muhammad Ali when he became the champ.

We all have a vested interest in the success of those from our hood who overcome adversities that most of us could not. No matter where they move or how famous they become, they will always be from our neighborhood. That's a lot of pressure for a young man or woman to handle but that comes with the territory of hood success. The problem is when they attempt to literally bring the hood with them. This quickly depletes their funds, as most of them are borderline illiterate to begin with, especially when it comes to finances. They make the money and give it right back to the very system that tried to oppress them in the first place. So before you know it, most of them are back in the hood, back in survival mode, back in the struggle. Using sports to advance in life is a competitive field nowadays. Parents from all walks of life and demographics see the benefit of using sports as a vehicle to pay for college via scholarships, so even on the peewee level, sports competition has become vicious. The only true difference is that in urban communities it could be a matter of life, death, or incarceration. So we play hard! But great athletes come a dime a dozen in the hood. There has to be guidance of the highest order to truly help an athlete with potential reach their apex. That's where a great coach comes in. He or she has to provide more than just the x's and o's of the game. They have to become life coaches as well. They may have to provide food, clothing, and sometime even shelter for those that they feel truly deserve it. They have to become fathers and mothers to provide nurturing far beyond the ball court. They have to be that guiding light when it appears to be the darkest. When a young man or women from the hood is provided with this type of foundation, the sky is the limit. Most fall short of receiving even half of what is required to make it, so they choose other paths. So we have to salute those coaches who go beyond the call of duty. We have to salute those fathers who not only look out for their own children, but also look out for the friends of their children who may not be as fortunate. We have to salute those mothers who get up early to make sure their child is on time to practice. Yes, sports are huge in urban America. Yes, sports have an artistic value to them. And last but not least, for those of us in urban America, sports are a way of life.

CHAPTER 13

THE ESPN AFFECT

This chapter is directly related to the culture of sports but I felt that it needed to be addressed separately. Long gone are the days when sports highlights were seen only on the 11 o'clock news or on Saturday afternoons. Now sports highlights are shown 24 hours a day, 7 days a week. ESPN has changed the landscape of sports in America forever. Coaches no longer have the power to teach the fundamentals of the game, or develop an athlete in stages to monitor his or her progression. Every athlete young and old now wants to bypass the learning stages of their development to go straight to the highlight stage. Everybody wants to be a star. As a result, they have become un-coachable. The athlete has been put on such a pedestal and glorified in such a manner, that they have been made to seem Godlike. ESPN has created an entirely new industry. Not just one that sells products, but one that sells ideas, concepts, pushes agendas, etc. The athlete it used to promote stories of success, failure, and crimes, even politics. The athlete's connection with young people of urban decent is only second to that of a rapper. They carry a lot of influence. This has a profound affect on the thinking and actions of urban youth. Their favorite athlete resides in their living rooms all day and night.

I wrote in my book Hip Hop Decoded that we have been cut off from the celestial stars that used to guide us and govern our lives, now we rely on man made stars for inspiration. We they rise, we rise, and when they fall, we fall as well. ESPN has helped to create this matrix where our youth have been emotionally, spiritually and physically aligned with athletes, even beyond sports. Our youth invest their life's energy in the journey of others. And truth be told, the experience is only real to the athlete since he or she is the only one playing. It's impossible for you, the spectator to truly know and feel what winning or losing a game of great magnitude is really about. Since you didn't put in the thousands of hours of hard work and practice leading up to a big shot or touchdown, your external experience is mere in comparison. However, being bombarded 24 hours a day 7 days a week with every aspect of a players life, ESPN has made it extremely hard for one to "unplug" from this artificial reality. With the notoriety provided by ESPN and other sports networks, sports is no longer everything, it's everything times everything. Even junior high school and high school players can see their highlights on the nightly sports news, and since basketball players can bypass college all together and still make it to the pros, it is the sport of choice for urban youth. But is the mentality of a high school athlete thrust into the limelight with millions of dollars and no true education a good thing? I beg to differ. ESPN had opened the fast track for urban athletes to excel by giving them maximum exposure at such an early age. As a result, we have multi millionaires who have not developed beyond a street mentality. Turn on ESPN these days and we are finally seeing the residual results of this process. We have begun to manufacture athletes at a quantum rate, and high schools, colleges, and corporate America are the biggest beneficiaries. There is an endless supply of athletes from poor environments that will line up to be exploited next, but I guess it beats standing on the corner, selling crack.

CHAPTER 14

FAST FOOD, SLOW DEATH

S oul food is the cultural cornerstone of urban America. Since the days of slavery it has been the one external constant that has kept us alive. Not just physically, but mentally and spiritually as well. However, the most important ingredient in soul food that has been overlooked for years is love, that's right, love. When you are given the worst parts of a pig and other animals to eat, but you know your survival depends on it, it takes a certain level of love to prepare, season, and cook food that would otherwise kill you and your family. Let's face it: besides the vegetables, there is absolutely nothing healthy in soul food. It is the direct cause of diabetes, high blood pressure, obesity, and any other sickness that you can think of. Yet and still, when placed in survival mode, nothing taste better, nothing fuels the body with more energy, nothing says home like a home cooked meal by grandma, and nothing brings the family together like soul food. Soul food is survival. Soul food is unity. Soul food is love. It has been taught to me by my elders that the auric field of the people who are cooking and preparing your food is very important. If they are not happy and filled with love, this could affect the food, and they can easily pass that particular energy into the food that they are preparing. That's probably why grandma's food would always taste the best. She always cooked with love.

Growing up in the early seventies, we knew nothing about fast food. And when it was finally introduced into the lexicon of the inner cities it was something that we got as a "reward" for graduating, winning a big game, or for other special occasions. Fast-forward to today and the situation is totally reversed. Now you only get a home cooked meal if you accomplish something extraordinary. How crazy is that? It was rather easy for fast food chains to set up in urban communities due to the lack of farms, trees, and grass. We were already living in a concrete jungle cut off from anything natural, so to introduce unnatural and artificial foods was easy. When you are cut off from nature, over the course of time, the body and biological make up of a person has to change and adapt to compensate. So the fast life of the city was priming us for fast food. Even the countryside would eventually fall victim to the fast food craze. Kentucky Fried Chicken was huge in the south. Even though it didn't reach the urban area until much later, it was one of the more successful franchises to catch on with Black people because it matched our frequency. We were already big fried chicken eaters, so when it was made and prepared and laced with the herbs and spices that we were already familiar with, we jumped at the opportunity to serve it to our families. Burgers and fries were a close second. As a child I was always fascinated at how meat could be made to look and taste like that. A very important factor to consider when we talk about the emergence of fast food is when mothers were forced or chose to leave the home to make a living. This had an immediate affect on the food that the children ate. Moms no longer had the time to prepare home cooked meal as often. So the convenience of fast food became a viable option. Some will say that this was a direct result the women's liberation movement of the sixties and seventies where women who felt that they were treated unfairly by men yearned to enter the work field and earn wages comparable to those of men. In terms of the African-American community specifically, most will say that as a result of black men being locked up or unable to find work due to discrimination or their lack of work skills, women from urban communities were forced to enter the corporate work place and provide for their families.

Remember, in urban communities family is everything, and soul food was the catalyst. I believe that it was a combination of things that led to the demise of soul food and the rise of fast food. Some may say that we traded one evil for another. That may be true, but at least with soul food, you knew exactly what you were eating. Your plate had potatoes, collard greens, macaroni and cheese, and meat. There were no chemicals or processed foods that you couldn't identify. So in addition to high blood pressure and diabetes, now we have been induced with foreign chemicals that have had an adverse affect on our bodies that we have yet to be able to fully diagnose. There is a chemical warfare being staged on everyone in this country but it is concentrated heavily in urban communities. On every corner there is a fast food establishment. From the Chinese restaurants (who knows what they are cooking?) to the more established fast food companies, we are under constant chemical assault. New studies have shown that chemicals in food can cause estrogen levels to be altered. When estrogen levels are too high in males, it forces them to act in a feminine manner. Could this be the cause of the rise of homosexuality in men? And if the rise in testosterone levels in women can also be attributed to the chemicals in food, could this be the cause of the rise of gay women? This I cannot substantiate, but it is worth us at least examining since we now have many studies that support the theory that vaccines which are filled with chemicals are causing many young children to exhibit signs of autism and other mental defects. So we have become a soulless people because the bond that was created by eating together was broken. It wasn't the food itself that nourished us. It was the love that was created by eating as a family that brought us through the toughest times. With that being said, when you know better, you do better.

The reemergence of vegetarianism has shed light on some of the health issues that we in the urban community have long suffered from. It has been said that we can reverse illness and aging if we go back to our natural state of being, which is being vegetarian. We need to go from soul food to "sol" food which is food cooked by the sun. I am a strong believer in this way of life. The problem is we no longer live in an environment that would fully support being a vegetarian. This is an urban jungle, and I believe that our biological make up has changed due to the high levels of stress and the fight or flight mentality of our urban environment. So we don't eat to live, we eat to survive. Now there even putting chemicals in the fruits and vegetables too! So fast food has become a reality, but it does nothing to bring the family together. It will never serve the purpose of soul food and it will never provide the spark of life like sol food. If we are what we eat, then we have become the guinea pigs of a new form of artificial intelligence. When we synchronize the food with the environment along with the virtual world that we now live in, it becomes easier to control the thinking of the people who partake in that reality. By disconnecting us from the food and the land, we have become spiritually disconnected as well. Urban warfare is real. Many of our young brothers and sisters seem to be heartless, emotionless, and unsympathetic. I believe the urban jungle in its totality – along with the lack of soul food – has turned them into the beast that we see today. As a result, this generation walks around devoid of soul. Never before has a generation of young people been so alien-like to our overall struggle to survive in this country. It's as if this generation is a new bloodline. They don't appear to be connected to our lineage. Could it be that the chemicals in the food have altered their DNA to create a new urban species? Well, if you talk to the elders in our community, I believe that they would say that this is highly possible.

CHAPTER 15

THE LANGUAGE OF "NAH MEAN"

(Do You Know What I Mean?)

T he English language is not our language so when we abuse it, it should not be looked upon as something negative but our DNA's attempt to recode it into something of spiritual value. The English language has very little if any spiritual power in it. We spoke many languages; Hebrew and Arabic are just a few of the more modern ones that still retain some of their power. On the continent of Africa there are literally thousands of dialects that are spoken, and there are new ones being created every day. As an ancient people we didn't speak for the sake of speaking. The pronunciation of every word had a purpose and a vibratory frequency to it. The tones of words were just as critical. Words change realities. The geometrical patterns formed when words are spoken properly can literally bring matter into existence. So the physical manifestation of life is formed by words and sound. Even in the Bible it states, "In the beginning was the word". Prophets come armed with nothing more than the word. Spiritual masters are able to lift humanity with powerful words of enlightenment. Motivational speakers are able to move crowds in positive directions with the right set of words. Reverends, Pastors, and Ministers are able to evoke the spirit of God within its followers by using inspirational words from a higher plane. Spoken word artists and emcees are able to entertain, inspire, and revolutionize the masses with words spoken in rhythmic patterns. Even pimps and hustlers also understand the power of the word, and use it to galvanize those who are in tune with that way of life.

Language is words spoken in a particular manner that is understood by a particular group. The meaning of words can be transformed when spoken in different languages. So it is not just the words spoken, but also the language in which they are spoken. Slang is a language that enables you to change the meaning of a word without changing the spelling of that said word. Words like "fresh', "dope", and "hot" when spoken in the language of Hip Hop had an entire different meaning than the standard English definition back in the days. These are words from the eighties that were coded within the language of Hip Hop, but coding words goes all the way back to slave times, maybe even before. Because English was forced on us, we were not equipped to access the spiritual faculties within ourselves by using it. We could not perform the rituals that we were accustomed to by using prayer and chants because we couldn't hit the right tones and frequencies using English to open up the portals to the spirit world. So as a people we were in spiritual lockdown. And the more fluent we became in using the English language, the greater the lockdown. How can you free yourself from your oppressor using his language and consequently his thinking? So we began to take what was linear (masculine) of the language and add some curves (feminine) to it. And in doing so, we breathed life into the dead spaces of the language and transformed it into something useful for us. No one can twist language the way Black people can. We are the original creators of language so once we are able to crack the code of a language; we can bend, manipulate, and alter it to suit our needs. For example, we can take a phrase like "do you know what I mean?" which is very linear, and bend it into "nah mean?" We can take the words "what is up?" and twist them into "s'up?"

The language is different but the intent is the same.

Our collective agreement in terms of the meaning of a word allows us to rewrite the code into whatever we want. If I say that the word bread now means money, and I introduce it into the lexicon of my immediate friends and family, who then accept it as such and begin to introduce it to their friends and so on and so on, we have collectively agreed that it is, so it is. In fact, the first secret society of the slaves was formed on the plantation using code words that were placed in songs. The words of these songs had multiple meanings that gave specific instructions on where to meet and what type of action was going to take place. Pig Latin was a language of broken and chopped words that was spoken by my mother and other adults when children were present. Until this day, there are certain words spoken in pig Latin that I still can't figure out. As we became freed men and women, we traveled throughout the country and took the science of twisting the language with us. As we began to express ourselves artistically, we started incorporating the secret language into our music as well. So we could play music that Europeans couldn't play and speak a language that Europeans couldn't understand. Over the course of time, each region would develop their own form of slang and language that was conducive to the people who lived there. However, if you were an initiate into the secret language, you could travel to any urban city in America and within fifteen minutes pick up on the dialect.

Dr. Robert Williams, an African-American psychologist, coined the phrase Ebonics to describe in great detail the science of our linguistics. Traditional educators cringe at the very sound of Ebonics, but we as a people always go with what we "feel" more so than what sounds right or what's proper. This is not to suggest in any way that one should not master the English language. We all should since coded within it are the keys that we need to free ourselves from under the "spell" of Europeans. The very word spelling should indicate that using this language properly could leave you confused. The saying "Good Morning" is a perfect example, since when is any mourning good? Hello or Hell is low in another. Laurel Airica is an amazing English linguist who breaks down the science of word magic and has done extensive research in this area. I would highly recommend studying her body of work.

The Bible is probably the greatest coded book in the western hemisphere. Reading it without understanding the language will only confuse you. Just as slaves used code words that had multiple meanings, Masons and other secret societies have mastered this, using signs and symbols as their primary language. What was once exclusive to us in urban America is no more. Rap music and urban dictionaries have exposed our secret to any and everyone. So now the new generation of urban teens have adapted text messages as their new language. They have found a way to abbreviate words in a unique fashion. Some leave out all of the vowels. It's a new form of Metu Neter, which is an ancient written language from Khemet that doesn't use vowels, or the vowels are interchangeable. It can be read left to right or right to left, etc. Short text is an official language simply because the youth have agreed to its existence. Most parents have not figured it out yet, but when they do, the youth will just create a new language to keep us in the dark. Rap creates new slang every day, and the means by which these words travel, via the Internet, social media, etc. is amazingly rapid. So at times it is hard to keep up. But if we as parents intend to keep the communication valves open with our youth, it is our duty to stay abreast of the ever changing world of language, "nah mean?"

CHAPTER 16

PRISON LIFE

Tthere are probably more spiritual people in prison than are walking the streets. This statement may seem crazy but the truth of the matter is when you look at the very infrastructure of America, how could there not be? America was founded on theft, deception, murder, disease, rape, etc. So when a people rebel against a system that is already void of spirituality, they are indeed closer to being spiritual than not. Think about it. Subconsciously they know that something is wrong so they are trying to break away and go against the grain in search of spirituality, only to find that there is none so they revert back to the very thing that they were trying to escape from in the first place. And as a result, they are punished. However, if you steal from a thief, is that really a crime? If you deceive the deceivers, how is that a crime? The only true crime is conforming to a system that is spiritually out of sync. This may sound confusing but I am just trying to illustrate that most people in prison have not broken universal law, but man made laws designed to keep the masses obedient. All while the law makers themselves break the very laws that they have created whenever they see fit. It's do as I say, not as I do. Now there are universal laws that should never be broken, such as impeding one's spiritual path. This means that everyone should have free will to be in tune with the most high without being deceived into worshipping false gods or manipulated into a world of evil for someone else's gain. It is also against universal law to take someone's life for no apparent reason. This does not apply to the animal world that kills for survival. However, when we have been turned into animals by being forced to live in an inhumane manner, killing becomes second nature. As a result, prisons all around the United States are filled with urban dwellers whose only true crime is following the blueprint of America to the letter, with the exception of getting caught. Let's face it: urban life is structured to produce prisoners.

Ever since slavery "officially" ended, a new form of slavery was created in order to maintain a system of order, population control, property protection, and fear among other things. This cannot be denied. As KRS ONE stated in his song "Sound of Da Police", the overseer became the officer. These revenue agents otherwise known as police officers are the frontline enforcers of creating revenue for the state. A constant barrage of arrests, fines, court appearances, and prison sentences orchestrates this. All which produce an extreme amount of capital for the state, Ferguson, Mo., is a perfect example. Even more important, the constitution doesn't apply to prisoners who are forced to work under slave labor conditions manufacturing goods for corporate America. So it's a win-win-win situation. The more prisoners, the more free slave labor, the more capital being generated, and the cycle continues. Creating the environment for future prisoners is not that difficult. The lack of education, jobs, two-parent households, and knowledge of self will inevitably create the criminal mindset that will eventually lead to a life of prison. Going to prison has become rites of passage for so many young black men and women in urban America. Most of us have friends and family members who are incarcerated as I speak. We cheer when criminals win because it demonstrates that they have not conformed and they are trying their best to defeat an already corrupt system. This is why when we go to the movies we root for the bad guys. So when prisoners come home, we applaud them for at least trying to beat the system, and when our young brother and sisters come home from college, we look at them with disgust because they have chosen to "sell out" to a system that has oppressed their people for years. How sick is that? Well, we are a sick people forced to live under sick conditions, so we breed sickness.

We are raised with the notion that prison is inevitable at some point in our lives. It is actually looked upon as major accomplishment if you can make it to your 21st birthday alive and without a prison record, while others success is measured by scholastic achievements, monetary milestones, or even military advancements. Over the course of many years of constantly being imprisoned fairly or unfairly we have become immune to the fear of being arrested and imprisoned. So the consequences of our actions rarely deter us from criminal behavior. Going to prison is now a self-sustaining process that runs on autopilot. We have become our own worse enemy. Prison is so deeply imbedded within our DNA that a new generation has been birthed with a straight to prison mentality. It is their destiny, because when young fearless warriors are birthed without the proper guidance and understanding of who the real enemy is and how to strategically attack, they will inevitably stage war against themselves and against society as a whole. They will bring this system to its knees or die trying. Knowledge of self and your true propose for being here is the only answer to breaking the code of mental and physical imprisonment.

Now for those who believe that I am making a bunch of excuses to justify the criminal behavior that takes place in urban America, you are absolutely correct. Under normal environmental circumstance where people are allowed to prosper in a fair and just system, it is highly expected of every man, woman, and child to govern themselves according to the laws of that particular land. Self-governing is the sign of a civilized community. Freedom, justice and equality are paramount if you truly want to achieve a highly civilized nation. If any or all components are missing, street justice, who manifests itself in many ways, will undoubtedly prevail. And this is what America is faced with on a daily basis. Those who have managed to govern themselves in a civilized manner under such duress know that at any given time that could all change. It is a thin line between school and prison, between work and crime, between life and death. So I applaud those who have figured out that America is the land of opportunity if you know how to navigate through the obstacles and pitfalls that are strategically placed before you. Yes, the odds are stacked against us, but more and more brothers and sisters are going to school, learning trades, following their dreams and succeeding. More brothers and sisters are adapting an entrepreneurial spirit and building their own companies. More young people are carving out their own niche in society as opposed to conforming.

So the future looks bright for those who choose to walk the straight and narrow, and for those of us in the urban community, we have to walk very straight and very narrow. With that said, this is still an uphill battle since most prisons are privately owned now and require that the prisons remain ninety five percent to capacity or face stiff penalties. So it is in favor of the state to arrest more people for what they consider "quality of life crimes", which is a code word for nothing at all. So for those who are so quick to pass judgment it is important to examine this from a panoramic viewpoint and take into consideration all of the evidence presented regarding the everyday struggle of those who live in an urban environment. Sure, we do a lot of harm to ourselves by not taking full advantage of all of the opportunities that are available to us in regards to free education, job programs, etc. However, one would only be scratching the surface in terms of how intricate the problems really are and who is also to blame. Everyone has to be held accountable, America for creating such a system designed to trap and incarcerate, and Urban America for sustaining such as system for so many generations.

Now that we have addressed the many pitfalls that lead to prison, lets take a look at the mentality one has to have when behind the walls. It is a world all its own. And unless you have experienced it first hand, it is really hard to put into words. However, we all have had family members, friends and associates who have been incarcerated so we have all heard the horror stories. From the death threats, sex threats, gang violence and gang initiation, ones spiritual arteries are easily hardened with a vile plaque of ill intent. It is a prerequisite for your survival to be able to defend yourself against all types of attacks, not just physical, but mental attacks as well. The strict ordinance by which one must comply, along with tense environment can break down the most hardened criminal. When you add idle time which is a vice, the inability to work out to relieve stress, or pursue a degree which is no longer allowed in prison, the mind begins to wander, and wander in the wrong direction. When you have a collective of minds that are on the same accord, the programming of ones thoughts are easily influenced. So over a course of time you are forced to think like a criminal, even if you are not one. This is usually balanced with the discovery of religion or a path to spirituality. Both are vying for the mental space that has all of a sudden become available due to the lack of physical movements. Whichever of the two that wins will manifest when that person is released back into the so-called civilized world. However, the longer that one is physically frozen in time, yet mentally able to travel way beyond the prison walls will inevitably create a reality that is not in synchronicity with the current matrix program that is running. In other words, your mental, physical, and spiritual software will have to be upgraded in order to survive beyond the walls. This is easier said than done. Those with great mental fortitude are usually the ones who can do their time without losing their mind. If one is not able to stay focused and make use of the time by learning a trade, having a strong spiritual foundation, and tremendous support from family and friends, then rehabilitation is highly unlikely.

The connections made behind the walls are just as critical. If your only connections are gang related, then chances are when you are released you will hit the ground running within that criminal organization. Let's face it: the ability to receive fair treatment in regards to finding legitimate work when finally released from prison is extremely low, if at all, so most have no choice but to return to a life of crime. As a result, the cycle continues. You return to prison as a repeated offender. You begin to feel more comfortable behind the walls where over the course of time you have formed a brotherhood with those facing the same adversity. Three hots and a cot are hard to pass up for those who cannot be assimilated and acclimated back into society in a progressive capacity. So on a subconscious level, they relieve themselves of the responsibility of trying to strive for something positive and allow the state to care for them. Or better yet, they come home and meet a woman that has to take care of them, depriving them of their manhood, and reducing them to nothing more than grown boys. The pressure to command respect inside the home as well as outside the home can be overwhelming. The street corner becomes a safe haven, drugs and alcohol becomes the outlet, and a return to prison is usually the end result. This is an intricate part of the culture of urban America, and until we change it at its root, it will continue to thrive.

CHAPTER 17

HAIR, NAILS, HANDBAGS AND SHOES...OH YEAH, IMPLANTS TOO!

This subject will be a very hard one for most women to digest, so I want to clarify from the beginning that I love an intelligent, confident, well-dressed, well-manicured woman. More importantly, I love a woman who has knowledge of who she really is well beyond her outer shell, and has a greater understanding of her role within the Black family and its pertinence to our survival. However, if we are going to deal with all of the issues that plague us in urban America, our women cannot be exempt from the scrutiny of their actions and how it affects us as a whole. This is my humble attempt to examine all that affects us when it comes to our urban lifestyle. And near the top of that list are our women and their irresponsible spending habits and negligence to things that are far more important than their physical appearance. The simplest way I can put it is hair, nails, handbags and shoes are to urban women what sneakers and cars are to urban men. The obsession to look good at all cost is a sickness suffered mainly by poor inner city women with high expectations but low self-esteem. This is a very bold statement to make, but when we examine the situation closely, what we see are urban women who look like a million bucks with no money in the bank or true equity to substantiate such a lifestyle. When your wardrobe doesn't match your bank account it points to even deeper issues.

These deeper issues may include but are not limited to the fact that our women may also be mentally, as well as spiritually bankrupt. As a result, looking good becomes the end all and be all. However, looking good at all cost becomes the ultimate detriment, especially for young women. For women of urban descent, these items are symbols of success, but they do not represent success itself. That requires a greater understanding of who you are beyond the material world. One of the first things a woman looks at when she meets a man is his sneakers, that's an urban fact! Well, men also have a checklist. They check for hair, nails, handbags, and shoes, in that order. It's sad that we view each other in this light, but this is a visual realm that we live in, so our ability to perceive beyond the physical has been greatly diminished by watching sports, reality TV, Rap videos, YouTube, etc. The perception of doing well is easy. We just have to look the part, and urban women are the very best at it. The rent could be late, but you would never know it. The refrigerator at home could be empty, but you would never know it. The children could need tending to but you would never know it. All is concealed in the hair, nails, handbags, and shoes. These items are used to insulate themselves from the stark reality that for most of them, it will get no better. Actually doing well requires them to be fiscally responsible in ways that they have not been trained in. Our financial priorities are backwards, so I am not blaming urban women for the conditions that they find themselves in when it comes to money. I'm simply stating that their ignorance to the financial potential that they possess has opened up a huge door for others to exploit.

This negligence has created a multibillion dollar industry that is owned and operated by Koreans who have created a monopoly when it comes to hair and nails. And let's not forget the billions spent on Italian handbags and shoes from high-end fashion boutiques. These are valuable dollars that leave our hood every single day with no reciprocation. It is imperative that we address the economic ramifications of such actions because it is our women who are more likely to master the economic system and help us get out of the financial doldrums that have hindered us for years. It is our women who are more likely to get a job in corporate America to learn the basic principles of finance. It is our women who are most likely to be put in a situation to learn the value of saving. And last but not least, it is our women who are most likely to even care about their credit score. And if you didn't know by now, your credit score is the new form of racism. If you have a very low score, it says that you are irresponsible, lazy, poor, and in some cases, untrustworthy. Those who are most likely to have a bad credit score are urban men and urban women who see the value of a handbag or some shoes as more important than building financially for the future. Not to make excuses for urban men, but most of them are off the grid to begin with since it's hard to find a job with a prison record, drug problem, disinterest in conforming to a corporate structure, or lack of valuable work skills that can easily be acclimated into a corporate environment.

Our women are well accepted in the work place so they at least have the economic potential to strengthen our communities and blaze a trail of financial independence that we all can benefit from when the time is right. In a perfect world, our men and women would both play an equal part in our development socially and economically. This is not a perfect world so the expectations of each gender will vary. Those willing to take on a greater role and responsibility to assist in our overall struggle must balance the unbalanced. This will most likely be the responsibility of our women for the reasons mentioned above. Our men will have to get out of the way and allow our women to lead us when it comes to matters of the money, but if their own priorities are not in order we don't have a chance. What does this have to do with hair and nails? well, everything. There is absolutely nothing wrong with looking good, but when every dollar that we spend empowers someone else, we have a major problem on our hands. Consumerism is another form of slavery. So while we are no longer in physical bondage, our economic impediment has created a new form of stagnation that has us chained to product consumption. This is not to be taken lightly. Everyone has a financial stake in us looking good, except us. Classism is another form of racism that is directly connected to our economic illiteracy. When a people do not control their financial destiny, they are preyed upon and discriminated against. So as we attempt to reclaim our position in society, we cannot overlook the importance of our economic disposition. So hair, nails, handbags, and shoes translate into billions of dollars that leave the hood everyday, along with the potential economic power that we possess along with it.

This is just the tip of the iceberg when it comes to this subject. Let's look at it from another perspective. The chemical process that takes place when woman put unnatural ingredients in their hair is irreversible. The lye alone can and does damage to the brain. The skin of your body is a living organism. It breathes and regenerates itself regularly. When you clog your pores with dangerous chemicals, it causes major damage to your internal universe. And when woman add the hazardous glue used in the fake nail tips, along with the chemicals in the food that they eat, it creates a very toxic environment. It is actually a testament of how strong the human body is to be able to withstand such abuse on a daily basis. Most urban women will not be seen without a perm in their hair. They then turn around and pass these same traditions of frying their hair down to their children at a very early age. As a result, the process, (no pun intended) continues for generations. The long lasting affects lead to cancer, thyroid tumors, and death. It appears that the risk is worth the rewards when it comes to looking good. I believe that most woman are not even aware of the immediate dangers of dyeing their hair, but have been programmed from an early age to do so just as their mother, sister, and aunts before them did.

The psychological effects of such actions are even greater. The longing to look European is at the forefront of such behavior. This goes all the way back to so called slave times when everything associated with being black was considered to be wrong. The straightening comb created by Annie Malone and inspired by Madame C.J. Walker was a breakthrough in terms of hair styling. Suddenly women could flatten and straighten their hair to give it that European look and feel. Being taught to hate you is a very powerful message that manifests itself in our everyday appearance. The so-called nappy kinky look was not accepted, especially in the work place. So, many women converted out of necessity, while most converted for sheer vanity. What one wears on their head represents their state of consciousness, so when we see our beautiful sisters wearing perms, dying their hair blond, and applying hair extensions, it means that they are of a European mind-set. Most women will not admit it; to them it is just a style. And I believe them when they say it, but I also believe that they suffer from an identity crisis as well. From a global perspective, it says to our African brothers and sisters who are on the outside looking in, that we have bought into the European way of thinking and that we do not identify with our ancestral ways, and our most famous women go to Hollywood and it seems that they have to perform some kind of sick blond hair ritual in order to get the approval of European producers and directors to get work.

Now some of the hairstyles that I see today represent neither African nor European, but are extreme in that they represent the chaos that is our thinking in urban America. Just head down to Atlanta for the annual hair show and you will see what I mean. I will admit that some of these bazaar looking hairstyles can be traced to our illustrious past, along with the first prototype for a straightening comb. On a subconscious level some women are in tuned with their ancient bloodline and choose to express that through the artistic approach of being creative, but most of them are not in tune and are just lost souls who will represent anything on their crown. In the court of public opinion, it makes us look uncivilized. When you see a woman with zippers, multiple colors, or even a fish bowl on her head, it makes us look savage-like. I know that these are the extreme cases, but these are the images that trend online for the entire world to see and pass judgment on us as a whole, not just the few who carry themselves this way. We have a long way to go in urban America to restore our image.

What most people don't know is that our hair is designed to be kinky and nappy for a reason. We have spiraling curls and coils that serve as antennas. These antennas pick up cosmic signals that keep us in tuned with the universe. I know that sounds crazy to most, but no part of our design is an accident. We were made perfect by the most high. Just look at a young mans head after he receives a very short haircut. What you will see will amaze you. At the top of his head, near the rear you will see that his hair design is spinning. Everything in the universe is spinning. Our planet is spinning, our blood in our bodies is spinning, and even when we flush our toilets, the water is spinning. So the spinning of our hair is an indicator of our connection to the universe. Our Jamaican brothers and sisters know this science all too well. Because we have been cut off from our culture, we have forgotten about this science and our connection to it. However, there has been a resurgence of women wearing their hair naturally. While some are doing it just as a fad, most are really in tune with their ancestors and their culture. Either way, the results are promising. It says that we recognized our beauty. It says that we have come to terms with who we are. It says that we know that our hairstyle has a greater purpose. The young ones follow our lead, so when the see us embrace our culture, so will they.

Now let's talk implants. Our women have stooped to a new low of self-hatred when it comes to desecrating their bodies for the sake of looking good. Never before have women who are already voluptuous felt the need to "improve" upon their appearance. Let's face it, Black woman already have big booties, how much more booty do they need? The answer to this question becomes irrelevant when we factor in urban women's fascination with reality shows, beauty magazines, and celebrities. These shows and magazines can make the most confident woman feel insecure. And when we add in the low vibration men who are only attracted to the physical attributes of a woman, her decision to destroy what is already perfect becomes an easy, yet detrimental one. The truth of the matter is that the emergence of the video vixen and the mainstream acceptance of the common stripper have created job opportunities like never before, the bigger the breasts and ass, the greater opportunity to make cash. So for those in the industry, it is just a business decision. However, for most women, they are just the byproduct of a new phenomenon called butt and breast implants. The advancements in science has made this procedure as simple as pulling a tooth. However, the cost of such procedure can become expensive, so woman of urban descent encounter greater risk because in a lot of cases they cannot afford a licensed doctor to perform the surgery. As a result they hit the black market and run the risk of getting a botched job done, or worse. Some women have even died. Some of the horror stories that I have heard and read about in regards to what is actually inserted into the buttocks will amaze you. Who in their right mind would do such a thing? However, our young urban women are not in their right minds so there is absolutely nothing that they are not willing to try to improve their appearance and opportunity to be seen and admired. If this type of effort were given to improving our personalities, love and respect for each other, and true knowledge of whom we are, then our world would be a much better place. Women are not the only guilty parties; men are now getting penis implants to enhance their bedroom performance. If we do not love ourselves then it is impossible for us to love others. We only attract that which we put out into the universe. So if we are only concerned about our physical presence, then one should not be mad when you only meet men who are attracted to your breasts, butts, or penis for that matter.

I truly understand the Europeans fascination with big butts and breasts. There was a time in London when they paraded a Black woman by the name of Sara Baartman around like she was some kind of circus freak because they were amazed at her body. They had never seen a woman so voluptuous before. Most European women at that time did nowhere near possess the physicality of the Black woman. As a matter of fact, when she died, they cut off her sexual organs and placed them in jars for spectators to see. So European women have always yearned to look African. It started with the vintage dresses that mimicked the big booty of the black woman. Now they get lip implants to mimic the fullness of our lips. And finally they have advanced to getting huge butts and breast implants to look even more Afrocentric. The most fascinating dynamic of this situation is while they are trying to look like us, we are dying our hair blonde trying to look like them. Talk about the irony of things. We should expect more type of implants in the near future as science continues to advance and we as a people continue to hate ourselves. We must also be on the lookout for new types of medical issues to arise as a result of us butchering our bodies.

CHAPTER 18

BARBER SHOPS, LIQUOR STORES, AND CHURCHES

These may seem like three separate entities on the surface but they are tightly embedded from a cultural standpoint. On Friday we head to the barbershop or the beauty salon, on Saturday we head to the liquor store, and on Sunday we head to church. One deals with our physical needs, one deals with our mental needs, and one deals with our spiritual needs. However, our spirit dwells in all three. The barbershop is the one place where you can gauge the spirit of the people. It is the place where you can get an honest conversation about a litany of subjects. The liquor store is the one place where you can ingest spirits in hopes of escaping the hardships of reality, even if just for a little while. And the church is the one place where you can catch the Holy Spirit in hopes of connecting with a higher power to make sense of all of the madness that has consumed us. We as a community use all three of these urban institutions faithfully. They are intertwined into our DNA. From an early age, these three pillars of urban society are instilled into the minds of our youth. They grow up experiencing all three at some point. So let's take a closer look at each and examine its importance from the perspective of urban culture.

Barber Shop / Beauty Salon

The barbershop is not just where you go to get a haircut, it's where most young men go to learn about sports, politics, women, drugs, crime, etc. It's the place where young men go to hear the elders from the community speak. The barbershop is where you get the raw, uncut truth about life itself. The greatest teacher is experience, so whenever you pull up a chair at your local barbershop, you become the student of a plethora of lessons that are being taught by the elders themselves. It doesn't get any better than that. It is one of the few legal black owned businesses in our neighborhood that has withstood every form of economic recession and every form of mental depression. There is a men's only meeting taking place every week across America, and it's held at your local barbershop. While this may not seem significant to most, for those of us who grew up without a father or a true male role model, this is the one place where we knew we were welcomed to learn and feel protected. And it is the one place that will also give young people a voice to express their own opinions and seek advice on the many subjects being taught.

The barbershop is a unique place where freedom fighters learn the true history of their great past, where political advocates receive their true degree in the science of how the game is really played in Washington, where religious enthusiast gather their first audience when teaching the word of God. It is where local artist sell their first cd's and get real feedback and criticism on if they are ready for the next level, it is where entrepreneurs receive their vision to be independent and the know how to make that vision a reality. It is where young hustlers get their game from the OG's, and the OG's keep their game sharp by listening to the young hustlers. And we all look good doing it. A packed barbershop on a Friday night is a good indicator that the economics in the hood is in a good place. This is when most men are just getting off from work, usually from a job that they despise because the treatment is three degrees better than a slave plantation. Nonetheless, they are "free" for the weekend to do as they please, so the first stop is usually the barbershop. This is where they restore their self-esteem. This is where they regain their dignity. This is where they are never treated less than a man. This is where their knowledge and wisdom is greatly valued. With the advances in technology and social media, every barbershop around the country should be linked so that our young brothers and elders can mobilize when the time is needed. So that true information can be shared without any propaganda from the media or other news sources. The same process takes place in the beauty salons for our young women as well. They learn the science of being women, their perspectives on men (good and bad), along with the gossip of the day, cooking recipes, etc. We have already discussed the economic ramifications of such behavior in the previous chapter, but for us, there are other spiritual benefits to congregating at such places that money cannot buy. The barbershop and beauty salons are the new underground railroads where our trek to freedom is more of a mental and spiritual journey than a physical one. We should hold such places in high regards and treat them with the sacredness and respect that they truly deserve. The library of Alexandria still exists within the spirit of our elders who reside right under our noses…in the barbershop.

There is an aspect of the barbershop from a cultural standpoint that must be addressed. That is that the barbers themselves are artist in their own right. They take great pride in their work of cutting, shaping, designing, and trimming hair. Some of their masterpieces can be very simple, and some can be very elaborate. The point that I am trying to make is that we cannot talk about culture without talking about art. They are connected at the seams. So, the gifted hands that transform one's face should not be overlooked. The tools of their artistry are clippers, straight razors, combs and brushes. The lines and curves that they carve into one's face are equivalent to carving a masterpiece into stone, or brilliant strokes of color across a canvas. The only difference is that your face is the canvas. When we are able to recognize the artistic value in everything that we do, we begin to realize that we are all artists in some shape, form or fashion and we are all performing on the stage of life in some capacity. However, after only being performers for so long, we need to now have aspirations of becoming the "directors" and "producers" of the show called life. That's where the true economic power is. When we own our artistry, we own our culture, which inevitably leads to owning our life. And the blueprint for such a game plan needs to be laid out, in the barbershop.

The Liquor Store

The crossroad between the barbershop and the church is the liquor store. We hit the barbershop to look good, and then we hit the liquor store to feel good. Or at least that is the plan on the surface. However, right below the surface is where the deeper issues lie, and the bottle of spirits is used to ignite or awaken the troubles that have been dormant from Sunday to Friday. The barbershop is where we deal with our general issues as a people; the liquor store is where we deal with our personal issues. These issues range from love and relationship, to work, to economics, as well as our overall living conditions. The bottle of spirits can activate a series of emotions based on your temperament at the time of ingesting it. The spirits can provide you with a fun and entertaining experience or a dark and revealing one. You are no longer in control of that destiny once you enter into the liquor store and choose a bottle of spirits to awaken. This process can be ritualistic in nature when done correctly. When the bottle of spirits is activated ceremoniously, the results are usually enlightening on a spiritual level. This is usually conducted under the guide of a master who understands the spirit world and how to the use the bottle to manipulate the gateways to that realm. The problem is that the ceremonial experience has been reduced to a party every single weekend in every city across America. The spirit guide has become the DJ or rapper that has not been initiated into the higher sciences of using the bottle of spirits in a way that will usually end on a positive note. As a result, only the darker, violent, sexual energy is activated.

The liquor store is neutral. The type of ceremony that you have will determine if your experience is negative or positive. It has been said that we are Gods having a human experience, which simply means that we are vessels of the most high and the experiences that we have in the physical teach God, which is beyond the physical about itself. Every experience will not and should not be positive, that would be countering productive, would it not? If the God in us is only allowed to learn about the positive side of itself, then we have only taught God about one half of the experience. That would be breaking the universal law of polarity, which states that if there is a positive there must be a negative. Drinking a bottle of spirits can be a part of the experience if you so choose. The problem occurs when we create a pattern of the same experiences called a habit that places the God within in a state of stasis. Another universal law is everything in the universe is moving, so the God within you must move and experience new things or the God within will die, leaving one with no choice but to manifest devilish behavior. Most of the problems that plague our community can be attributed to us not mastering that bottle of spirits. We become violent, we become abusive, we become depressed, we become reckless in our sexual endeavors, and oh yeah, living the same experiences over and over, we become alcoholics, so entering a liquor store should not be taken lightly, especially for young people who have not yet mastered their emotions, and whose thoughts at that age are focused on two things; partying and having sex. They haven't banked enough experiences in other walks of their life to balance out the dangers of activating a bottle of spirits without consequence. As a result, most teenaged drinkers make bad decisions while under the influence that they will regret for the rest of their lives. The older people who have been drinking since childhood have created patterns that are so deeply embedded within their psyche that they have actually written their own program of destruction that runs on the operating system of this universe. They only way to correct such behavior is to upgrade the operating system, which is easier said than done.

There is also an artistic connection to the liquor store as well. As I stated earlier, I am not writing this book to be politically correct, I am writing it to be realistically correct, meaning we have to deal with was is going on as opposed to what we wish was going on. Many artists, but recording in particular summon the spirit world to tap into their creative forces. Some meditate, some use drugs, but one of the more common practices is activating a bottle of spirits to open up that creative vortex within themselves. This is a practice that has been going on for hundreds of years. As I mentioned earlier, the bottle of spirits will amplify your temperament, so if you are in a creative mode, chances are the alcohol will assist you in bringing that creativity out of you. Yet remember, it is not the use but the abuse of the spirits that can cause you harm. The practice of using the bottle to activate creativity is usually a trait of the neophyte. When one becomes a master of the creative realm, they understand that you can secret into the bloodstream the same enzymes that produce the experience of having drink. That's where the true magic lies. When you no longer need external stimulants to achieve a creative euphoria, then you have truly tapped into the God within. Until then, the liquor store will always serve as a place to activate such forces.

The Church

The church brings this process full circle, but let's not forget that a circle is also a pattern. Running in circles creates grooves that become deeper and deeper the longer that we run. It's like carving a circle pattern on a table with a knife, then placing a marble in between the grooves. Initially the marble would be able to easily escape the grooves because they are not that deep. However, the deeper the grooves become based on the circle pattern that we create; it becomes very hard for the marble to escape. The marble is symbolic to our spirit being trapped deep within the patterns of our drinking, smoking, sexing, eating, and other negative behaviors. This is where the church comes in. In order for the marble to escape the pattern of the circle, it must spiral in an upward motion out of it. It must move from a two dimensional function to that of a three dimension function, which is on a higher plane. It must raise its vibrational frequency through its understanding that it is more than physical, but spiritual. The true purpose of any church should be to teach the science of spiraling by way of ascension above the negative patterns that we have created in our physical lives. Any and everyone who want to find their connection to the all can access this spiraling stairway to heaven. The true purpose of any church should also be to teach that God dwells within each and every one of us, and that we all have the ability to climb, or raise ourselves out of the depths of hell, into the kingdom of heaven. If this is not the standard practice of the church that you attend, then you should run! Just as the liquor store can amplify the spirit, the church is the ultimate spirit amplifier.

The ceremony of song, dance, and the word of God serve as the launching pad of the spirit. Unfortunately most churches today are not spirit raisers, but spirit catchers. These spirits become trapped because the church itself does not follow its own spiritual principles. It has become just as corrupt as any other organization. The ones who are supposed to lead by example have fallen victim to the same circumstances as its congregation. Church is big business in the urban community. However, the church served a greater purpose for those of our elders who were slaves. Not all of our ancestors arrived here on slave ships, but for those who did; the church served a very important role of restoring hope. After being robbed of our name, language, religion, culture and God, the church was the only place where we could gather to sing, dance, and mimic some semblance of the magic that we had not forgotten, to raise our energy beyond the physical. Unfortunately we had to use the slave masters blueprint (Bible) and under the guise of the slave masters blonde haired blue eyed God to do it. However, even in our lost state we still understood that spirit was spirit, and the Jesus figure that the slave master praised was only a sigil that our ancestors used to thrust themselves into the spirit world. In the beginning they did not literally believe in the slave masters God, but they understood it from a symbolic standpoint. The slave master worshipped the "Son" of God, our ancestors worshipped the Sun of God, The slave master taught that Jesus was the light of the world, our ancestors knew beyond a shadow of a doubt that the sun was the light of the world.

The slave master taught that Jesus gave his life so that we may live; our ancestors knew that the sun gave off its energy and light to grow vegetation, regulate the atmosphere and control water so that we too may live. The slave master also taught that Jesus had 12 Disciples, our ancestors studied the heavens and knew that there were 12 constellations that moved around the sun, and based on their characteristics they named them after certain animals like bulls, rams, fish, scorpions, or certain archetype symbols like water, virgins, scales. And isn't it ironic that even the slave master worships his God on Sunday? After hundreds of years of being beaten, tortured, murdered, raped, castrated, and burned, Jesus took on a whole different meaning for our ancestors. Just as torture victims do, our ancestors created an alternate reality in their minds to escape the physical pain. And since Sunday was the only day that they were "free" of such torture, Jesus became synonymous with being their savior, and this leads us back to today. We are still under the same spell, and the sad thing about it is, even after all of the horrible things that the slave master did to our ancestors, including lynching's, divide and conquer, and all of the other atrocious things previously mentioned, we still believe that the one thing that he gave us that was pure, innocent, and true was his God. Yes, we are a sick people. This is why there is very little, if any magic left in the churches, mosques, or synagogues. Yes there is dancing and singing and a symbolic rising of spiritual energy, but no real spiritual magic.

The spirit within has been programmed in a downward spiral deep into the realms of matter and the laws that govern it. Even the church has succumbed to the realm of the material. These mega churches are raking in millions, and right outside of them the people are basically starving. As a result there has been an exodus of young people from the church who don't believe in its power. This new generation of young people is asking valid questions about life, God, and their existence beyond this physical world, and they are not receiving the answers that they are looking for, at least not in the church. There is a reason that there is a barbershop, liquor store and church on just about every corner of every hood in America. They represent the circle pattern that we continue to run in but find very hard to escape. We go from looking good (barbershop), to feeling bad (Liquor store), to spiritually lost (church).

CHAPTER 19

VAMPIRES OF THE CULTURE

I would be remiss if I didn't mention the vampires who suck the life out of our culture. These vampires do not live in our neighborhoods, yet they set up shop and systematically feed off of the caucus of the people. This is all done under the guise of providing a service that the people need. However, most of the services provided are detrimental to our cause or are of such poor quality that they do more damage than good. These vampires are out for blood, not the physical blood that runs through our veins, but the economic blood that runs through our communities. No matter where we go, there they are. The stronger they become, the weaker we become, financially. And when the economic power of a people has been compromised, they function as slaves. These vampires are of different breeds and races and they don't always agree with each other, but they have a collective agreement amongst themselves that they must keep their heel on the necks of the urban communities. The economic pulse of the community rises on the first and fifteenth of every month. This is when the hood is most vibrant and alive. We receive an economic boost of energy and these vampires are right there with an "IV" access to drain the overage. By the time that they finish feeding, we are left with barely a pulse.

The Chinese Restaurant

SubAllow me to preface what I'm about to say by stating that this is not a racist rant. It is a cultural observation of what I see when they step into my neighborhood. The Chinese restaurant is a part of our culture, but it is a part of the culture that doesn't add on to the culture or enhance the culture in any way. Its contributions to the culture actually hinder its progress. In every urban neighborhood there is a Chinese restaurant, but the ironic thing is that most of the food that they cook and serve is not Chinese food per se. It is actually food that plays on the stereotype of what we, the urban community think Chinese food is. Just like four chicken wings and pork fried rice is a concoction created by the Chinese based off of the stereotypes that they have of our eating habits. Beyond the obvious fact that the food being served has no nutritional value, the synergy created when eaten does not connect us to who we are from a cultural standpoint. This is critical because food is also information.

When we eat something that connects us with our homeland or reminds us of our culture, it empowers us spiritually. It enables us to keep our heritage alive, even in a foreign land. So when another culture sets up shop in our neighborhood and serves us hybrid food, it creates an even greater disconnect from our own culture. Poor people suffer the most when this happens. Economically they are looking for the greatest value for their dollar, and the Chinese restaurant provides that. However, poor people are also the most disenfranchised in any community as well, so more than anything else, they need their food to provide cultural identity as well as nutritional and economic value, and that's asking a lot from an outside culture to provide. It's one thing to experience someone else's culture and food, it's another thing to have to rely on it for your own survival, and our poor business practices have limited our ability to provide the necessary services that our own people need to thrive, not just survive, the more someone else's culture that we embrace, the more of our own culture that we will forget. As a result, we have a race of people who are lost, and a race of vampires who continue to feed off of their ignorance.

The general consensus among Chinese people when it comes to so-called Black people is that they are lazy, savage, criminal, and dangerous. Where would they pick up such ideas from? Could it be the media's portrayal of us via the news, or Hollywood's portrayal of us as pimps, hustlers, thugs, whores, etc? Maybe it's our own doing when we put out rap videos and reality TV shows that show us in a negative light. All of the above are responsible and contribute to these stereotypes. Even the movie and rap videos, which can be seen as artistic expressions from our viewpoint, are seen as realistic depictions of who we are by those outside of the culture. They take these images literally! So those Chinese people who are brave enough to enter our neighborhoods, albeit through strong plexiglass have one thing on their minds; get the money and get out! And it's sad to say that the way we act only reinforces what they have been told about us in the first place. When the urban community truly learns the importance of their economic power in their own communities, then, and only then will we spend money with those who respect our culture. Being robbed of our true culture we have morphed into an entirely new one that has incorporated every other culture as a substitute for our own. As a result, we don't know who we are.

Italian Restaurant/Pizzeria

The same concepts apply when we talk about Italian people and the restaurants, pizzerias, construction businesses, and other ventures that they open up in poor neighborhoods filled with non-Italian people. They too are a very proud culture and have very right to be. However, their perception of us from urban areas is no different than that of the Chinese. What I find facetious is the fact that most Italians have black blood running through their veins as a result of the Moors ruling Spain and Italy for hundreds of years, mixing and mingling with the people of that region. This is why some of them have kinky hair similar to that of so-called black people. Even their mannerism would suggest that they have a little "Moor" soul in them, (pun intended). To most of them, Black people are nothing more than "Moolies" or "Mulunyans", which is a derogatory term, which mean eggplant in Italian. Uncooked eggplants are black. Still in all, they set up shop and do business. When an Italian sits down to eat food at one of their restaurants they immediately connect with their culture and feel empowered doing so. Even those who have never actually been to Italy still are reminded of a place where their ancestors derived from. This is not to suggest that Italians do not open up businesses or service their own communities because they do and very well I might add, but the very word community in essence means "common unity", which mean that they are all on the same page about who they are and will do whatever they have to, to preserve their culture. Nonetheless, when you enter into someone else's community, I feel that the energy exchanged should be reciprocal.

Very rarely are we allowed on their construction sites, or they make it very tough to get into their unions, rarely do you see us working in their restaurants beyond a servitude role, rarely are we employed by their private sanitation firms, hell, we can barely get work in their organized crime cliques. So what services do they truly provide to urban communities, the food? Well we already know that starches, sugars, flour, etc. are not conducive to people of color. All food is good in moderation, but over the course of consuming these ingredients, they have contributed to our high obesity rates, high blood pressure, diabetes, gout, etc. So they too, are complicit in our downfall as a community. Nonetheless, the biggest perpetrators of our demise from a cultural standpoint are we for allowing others to set up shop and take advantage of our non-cultural identity.

The Arabs

It is against Islamic law to eat pork or ingest alcohol, but in every urban neighbor that they set up shop, the Arabs sell these products to us on a daily basis, why? The easy answer to this question is to say that it is the individuals choice to consume such products, and that the Arabs should not be held liable for such actions. That would be politically correct, but I believe that the answer to this question is much deeper. Our relationship with the Arabs did not begin here in North America. They are partly responsible for the slave trade that brought many of our ancestors to this country in bondage. I say partly because there were many conspirators including Africans themselves, but the Portuguese were the first to engage in buying and selling Africans. When they landed on the shores of Africa they didn't speak the language of the people, so they used the Arabs as an intermediary between them and us. The Arabs spoke our dialect and they were paid very well by the Portuguese to set up meetings with tribal chiefs, and the rest is history.

The Arabs are original people who know the true history of so called Black people. They know that we are the oldest people on the planet, they know we built the pyramids, they know that we are the mothers and fathers of science, geometry, medicine, astronomy, etc. They know that Islam is an African religion, which they have been fortunate to partake in. They also know that as a result of the slave trade that most of us who were brought here against our will are disconnected from our illustrious past. So to take advantage and exploit us would not be that hard. Meanwhile, back to America. They do not hire us to work in their stores, they talk down to us as if we are subhuman, and the language barrier creates an even bigger disconnect between them and us. If you are from the hood you know this to be a fact. They are only here for the American dollar and we represent the easiest way to get it. Based on the harmful products that they continue to sell us, including tobacco, they do not consider us their brethren. Even though we are "cousins" based on the proximity of our birth land, the despise that they have for us as a people is clearly apparent. Can we really blame them? We have to take responsibility for bettering our condition through righteous actions. Those actions include the way we conduct ourselves at all times, regardless of our economic status, religious beliefs, or political stance. When we treat ourselves better, others will have no choice but to fall in line and respect us as an equal contributor to society. Until then, we will continue to be the victims of exploitation at the hands of other cultures.

The Koreans

As mentioned in an earlier chapter, the Koreans have a stronghold on the artificial hair industry. Even though there is a new trend of urban women wearing their hair in a natural state, most still rely on weaves and extensions. These trends are set by women in Hollywood, music artist, video vixens, and athletes, and most of them have blond weaves, or very expensive extensions. This is a $4 billion dollar a year industry and urban women are at the mercy of the Koreans who have monopolized it. When you walk inside of one of their establishments you can immediately feel the tension as we are scrutinized as potential criminals. There is also a language barrier. It's a very strange relationship where they need us, but they hate us at the same time. Koreans have no known historical connections to people in urban areas, so they are only there for the financial gain.

The Africans

Yes, the Africans. For some strange reason, the Africans who migrate to America do not see us as their brethren. They too see us as savages and animals. I was told by a very reliable source that when they are entering America, they are instructed to watch an orientation video on how to deal with, and understand people from urban areas. This process is very similar to when someone's going to the zoo and has to be instructed not to feed, stay away from, or beware of the dangerous animals. In some instances African merchants treat us worse than other foreigners. However, we do have a genetic connection with Africans that is stronger than all other so-called foreigners. I feel that they should have more compassion considering they understand our journey, or they should understand our journey since they are partially responsible for it. We are the "lost" tribe that was forced into slavery, losing all previous knowledge of our great past. Those who came over on slave ships did not ask to come here. Africans hold the key to us re-"membering" our past. Their arrogance when it comes to us is strictly based on the fact that they know who they are. And yet they still treat us like dirt. We have a lot to offer each other. As they continue to acclimate themselves to the American way of life, who better to assist them in this process? Who better than us to help them navigate through the terrain of American culture? Who better than us to prepare them for the racial discrimination that they most likely will face in this country? So while they hold the key to our past, we hold the key to their future, in this country at least. Most Africans come to this country and are awestruck by the many opportunities that are afforded every citizen. It literally baffles them at our inability to take advantage of these privileges. America has free education, free food programs, low income housing with running water, free speech, and a host of other free programs and services that Africans could only dream of in their home country.

This is not to suggest that Africa does not have these luxuries and opportunities. Some of the countries have this and then some, but the ones that come here looking for a better way of life despise us because we have not taken full advantage. They see us as very lazy. And for the most part they are right. They are able to come to this country, work twice as hard as we do, go to school at night, save money, easily get a loan or a line of credit, and open up their own businesses, all while maintaining a sense of their dignity and culture. And when we, the "urbaners" walk into their establishment, we are treated like common criminals. We are treated as if we do not belong. And even though our blood, sweat, and tears built this country, we are below the African in status, simply because we do not know or identify with our culture. What the African has not taken into account is that the reverberation of over 400 years of physical, mental, and spiritual trauma afflicted upon us is still prevalent today. These actions have forced us to act other than ourselves. As a result, we do not resemble a people from the same lineage, bloodline, or have the same DNA running through our veins. So yes, our relationship with our African brothers and sisters is complicated. Then there are those who will say that we should get over it. Slavery was over 400 hundred years ago and we should just move on. To them I say, the Jewish community has never gotten over The Holocaust, and they never should. It changed the course of their history. The big difference is that they were able to migrate to a different land with their history intact. Therefore, the rebuilding process became a little easier. And even though there was a lot of death and torture in the concentration camps, the history, culture, language, and religion of the Jewish people was not taken from them. Africans come to this country with those essential building blocks in place, so they just have to adjust and adapt to the American way.

The Jewish Community

We Urban Americans can learn a lot from the Jewish community. The way they run and operate their own businesses, the way that they finance their own security teams to protect their own communities, their ambulance services that aid their sick and elderly, and their synagogues to teach and preserve their religious beliefs is nothing short of extraordinary. Their supreme understanding of economics is fascinating as well. They look out for their own. In fact, The Jewish dollar doesn't leave their communities until it has circulated at least twenty times. Think about that for a second. At the root, they are building and supporting their businesses before they even attempt to patronize any other establishment that is not Jewish. The African-American dollar leaves our community immediately, and when I say immediately, I mean within hours! The Jewish community provides their own food, which is kosher for them to eat, and their own schools to teach and educate their young as well. This is what you call power. Now, with that being said we must address the "elephant" in the room when it comes to Jewish people in relation to those of the African-American community. Due to the teachings of the Torah and their overall religious beliefs, Jewish People feel that they are the chosen people of God, and they act like it when it comes to how they treat all others who are not Jewish. I am not suggesting that they treat all other races bad, they are very respectful to those who treat them accordingly. However, any relationship that you establish with the Jewish community is strictly about business in some shape form or fashion. You are not allowed to attend their Synagogues, schools, and their ambulance service will not pick you up in your time of need. This may not be technically factual, but where I'm from this couldn't be more evident. And if you so happened to walk into one of these establishments, you most certainly will not feel welcomed.

So the relationship between those in the urban community and the Jewish community is that of consumer and provider, boss and worker, tenant and landlord. We do not follow the Jewish faith, but two or three times a year our public schools are closed to acknowledge and celebrate their holidays...and their children do not even attend our schools. Their presence is prominent in the urban community. They own most of the real estate and most of the retail businesses in the hood. Even though they might not have much of a physical presence because they hire individuals who look like we do to manage their urban affairs, they reap the benefits of the urban dollar. They too have gotten their hands dirty during the slave trade, which no one seems to want to talk about. So everyone that benefits off of the economics of the hood has been complicit in some way. Many are responsible for our demise and inability to reestablish us as a respectable people in this country. So we must learn from the way that others treat us, and better yet how they treat themselves and their interest when it comes to urban affairs. By doing so, we will become stronger economically, spiritually, politically, and socially.

I want to reiterate that this is not a racist rant or me playing the victim card about all that is wrong with the urban community without taking responsibility for our own affairs. It is not about all that is right or all that is wrong. It's about all that is, simple as that. The economics of the hood is being syphoned away by other racial and ethnic groups at an alarming rate. And while that is not a crime per se, because we do live in a capitalist society based on free enterprise, there is a moral responsibility to deal fairly, the way that others deal with Urban America borders on the line of operating in a predatory nature. In this society, if a people have no economic power, then they have no power. Economic power leads to political power; political power changes conditions. There are those who will quickly pull the race card or try to incite confusion about what I am saying. Those are the ones who are stuck on delusional and not the facts regarding who holds the economic power when it comes to Urban America. All that I am doing is painting a vivid picture of the landscape of the hood from as many perspectives as I can. When we step outside, this is what we see. This is who we spend our money with. This is who governs our streets, legally and illegally. This is who owns the property in which we reside, etc. etc. etc. I truly respect all other races and cultures that we interact with on a daily basis, but they are not coming from where we are coming from, literally or figuratively. So we need time to rediscover our greatness, we need time to understand the basics of finance, we need to develop a sense of business savvy, as well as an overall willingness to learn how to empower ourselves socially and spiritually. I believe if given the opportunity to do so, we will thrive just as much as all other groups who currently occupy our communities.

CHAPTER 20

RAP IS MY SAVIOR

This may be the most sensitive topic that I will cover in this entire book but it needs to be addressed because it has this generation of artist and aspiring artist on creative lockdown. Seven out of ten people that I know on a personal level in this day and time are rappers, aspiring to be rappers, claim to be rappers, are soon to be rappers, are old school rappers making a comeback, or are coming out of prison with a dream to become a rapper. Everybody, and I mean everybody is a rapper now. How is this even possible? What has taken place over the last twenty years that would give the average person the urge and desire to want to get involved with rap, and get involved on a level that borders on the fence of obsession? The operative word here is "average". As you will soon come to find out, it doesn't require much more than an average skill set to succeed in the rap industry. Young people in particular are willing to abandon their pursuit of education, learning a trade, or even learning the basics of music in the traditional sense to pursue rap. Their dreams begin and end with the pursuit of a rap career in some capacity, whether it's rapping itself, producing, modeling, dancing, a radio personality, or making rap videos. For them, the ends outweigh the means, and the rewards far outweigh the risk. Even sports have taken a back seat to rap because sports still require practice, dedication, and superior skills to advance. Their actions and ways of thinking are justified every time a new talentless artist emerges with a hit song fueled by a hot beat and some rudimentary rhymes that goes on to sell a million copies and makes them a household name. Meanwhile, parents, educators and elders keep stressing the importance of going to school to get a good education so that you can one day land a job that will pay you about $60,000 a year if you are lucky. Meditate on that for a moment. If you were a young urbanite who grew up very poor with a limited education, resources, opportunities, yet you had an opportunity to rise above these conditions without the need for a specialized skill or degree, and could make millions of dollars traveling the world as a famous artist, what would you do? After being looked at from this perspective, I believe that the answer becomes very clear on what we are facing with this generation of youth and those who live in urban America in particular.

Rap is their savior. However, when everybody can rap, nobody can rap. I will say that again, "when everybody can rap, nobody can rap". When an art form of any sort has been overexposed, oversaturated, or exploited it loses its power. It becomes mundane. The mere fact that everyone feels like they can do something suggest that is doesn't really require much skill at all. This is why I always differentiate between emceeing and rapping. Emceeing requires a tremendous amount of skill, knowledge, breath control, insight, vocabulary, stamina, stage presence, etc. These attributes are not necessarily required to rap. An emcee can rap, but rarely can a rapper emcee. Now don't get me wrong. Rap has its place. I will be the first one to tell you that I enjoy a great rap record from time to time. Yet in the grand scheme of things, the rap industry does not enhance or add anything of value to our culture as a whole except money and fame. And for those who have been deprived of basic necessities in life, that's more than enough! Now there will be many people who are quick to ask, well, what's wrong with that? And my answer would be, nothing at all. Just don't complain when you see rappers on television with their pants hanging off of their ass if they are male, or half naked with a thong up their ass if they are female. Just don't complain if most of their lyrics are disrespecting women, or selling drugs, or killing other people. Just don't complain when they make Black people look like savages overall. Know and understand that it is just for the money and fame. It all boils down to economics. The path of least resistance to making it out of the hood is through the rap industry. It is very easy to do and the profits can be astronomical.

Let's be clear, the rap industry feeds a lot of people. So the resistance that one will get when attempting to uncover what may be wrong with it will be strong and fierce. Any venture that provides food, clothing, and shelter, whether legally or illegally that is being criticized, will be met with skepticism, ridicule, and contempt. I am in no way trying to shut down the rap industry or deny anyone an opportunity to feed his or her families. I am only appealing to the higher consciousness of those who have the capacity to reason beyond the financial benefits of the industry and examine the totality of the industry and its effects on this generation and future generations to come. The financial progress of a few can lead to the spiritual and cultural decline of the whole. Herein lies the heart of the dilemma. And that selected few is not limited to just the artist themselves, there are those who have worked hard to earn a degree in business, or are certified to engineer a session, or have graduated with a degree in videography who also have to accept responsibility. These are the behind-the-scenes people but their role in the progress or demise of rap is just as significant. Every time that a DJ plays a record that he or she knows is garbage, every time a videographer shoots a video that they know doesn't show us in a good light, or every time an interview is conducted that we know should never see the light of day, we are complicit in the destruction of the culture of Hip Hop for the sake of making money in the culture of rap, it's just that simple. Yet it's the only way to survive in the industry. If a DJ works for a radio station, then the program director basically tells him what to play. After hearing the same terrible song on the radio a hundred times, you somehow begin to like it, or tolerate it at best. Now that same DJ who wouldn't dare play such records on his own time is forced to give the people what they have been programmed to believe is hot. The same thing goes for the video director who is instructed to direct the same video for just about every artist that the label pays him or her to shoot. You know the video, girls barely dressed, guys pouring champagne, fly cars, nice jewelry, wads of cash, and cut! Ninety five percent of all rap videos will have all or at least a variation of these elements in them. Even though the video director may be talented and has a vision that would broaden the scope of most rap videos, they will simply do what they are paid to do in the long run. Rap allows most artists to mask their illiteracy or inability to function beyond a hood mentality, and it allows them to do so without apologizing since in most cases they make more money than the average college graduate.

No one is going to stand up for what's morally right in terms of how we are portrayed or the effects that rap has had on the minds of young men and women because making money at any cost has become the new standard of what's morally correct and what isn't. The rap industry has provided a better way of life for a lot of people, so who am I to even suggest that it is not good for us? For those of you who have the vision to see beyond the fame and fortune you know exactly what I am talking about. Through the eyes of rap, police officers respond to us differently, judges sentence us differently, teachers reprimand us differently, the media portrays us differently, and even the elders of our culture treat us differently. Because of our association with rap, in most cases by default, it makes us guilty of the ways and actions portrayed by a small few in the name of making money, but under the guise of creative expression. Most of that is wrong with rap culture is cloaked in these terms "creative expression", and "freedom of speech". This enables those who are at fault to escape liability for their actions. Every time that there is an uproar from the general public regarding the foul language, negative portrayal of women, or violence rapped about or displayed in rap videos, a rap industry front man will appear to quell the disturbance by hiding behind freedom of speech verbiage. One of the biggest statements made by artist themselves is "you should monitor what your children listen to because we are not responsible". This is what I call straight bulls***! Most of them know that if parents were able to truly monitor what their children watched and listened to that most of these subpar artist would not even exist, and that is a fact. They are banking on our inability to monitor what our children are watching and listening to. Their careers literally depend on it.

Sex, drugs, and violence are a product like any other product being sold on the open market. The goal of the company selling it is to make as much money off of this product as possible. It has nothing to do with being creative or cultural, or morally correct. Most of these record executives are not culturally in tuned with the music that they are selling, so they never factor in whether it will have residual effects on its clients. Their goal is to satisfy their shareholders every quarter. So when we protest that there is not enough balance on the radio, or not enough songs with positive messages, we miss the entire point, and that point is making money. We also like to demonize the industry by stating that they have an agenda to promote a certain negative lifestyle to our children, and that may be true. However, the root of their intentions, at least on the surface is business related, nothing personal. If you can understand this, then everything else will make sense. It is not there responsibility morally to put out music that is conscious, educational, cultural, and non-violent, etc. Do you really think Pepsi is concerned about the diabetes rate of young people in America? Do you really think the Tabaco industry cares about the cancer rate skyrocketing as a result of their product? And more importantly, if you were a young executive working for one of these companies and you had a mortgage to pay, college loans to pay off, and two car notes every month, would you care about the moral responsibility of such things, or would you be doing your best to ensure that these quotas were met? The executives who work for the music industry are no different. We as a community tend to take everything personal. We look at everything as a personal attack on our well-being and way of life. This is called victim consciousness.

The truth of the matter is these boardrooms are filled with executives who could care less about your ethnicity, race, religion, sexual preference, or lifestyle. As long as you buy their products they get paid. Now apply this concept to the rap industry. Why would any executive bring out a new artist or song every time you wanted to hear something new? Here is the undeniable truth; there are only twelve to fifteen slots available and a million rappers trying to fill them. Any corporation would collapse overnight if it followed a protocol of releasing a new product every three months or so. KFC doesn't change its ingredients to its famous fried chicken… ever! It is their flagship product. They may grill it, barbecue it, or bake it, but the formula remains the same. So when you look at sex, violence, drugs, and even controversy as a product, you get a better understanding of how the industry is set up. Even the devil worship, illuminati rumors that swept through the industry a few years back was about money. Conspiracy theorist created such a buzz that executives and managers saw an opportunity to capitalize off of the situation, and instructed their artist to wear or display symbols that were associated with devil worship or the occult realm just to garner a reaction. As a result, certain artist became hot topics and they eventually sold more records. This only demonstrates that the industry is reactionary as well. So if "conscious" Hip Hop started creating a buzz with the masses, these record labels would find a way to put them in position to reap the benefits financially.

Now, with that being said, if you have read my previous works called "Hip Hop Decoded", you know that I strongly believe that there are levels to this that is far beyond the comprehension of most peoples understanding with respect to the recording industry that has absolutely nothing to do with money. So my stance on mind control, occult signs and symbols, and other esoteric principles regarding music has not changed. However, this is a book about how the rap industry has become a part of the culture of Urban America. This is a book about how the rap industry has been embedded deep within the psyche of millions of young urbanites that are willing to give up the pursuit of everything else for a shot at making it in the industry. Most of them view this as their only way out and they will stop at nothing to attain this goal. The rap industry is an institution unto itself. It provides an economic base; a social base, an artistic base, a spiritual/religious base, and these are just some of the more critical components of a culture as a whole. The rap culture/industry is self-sustaining now. You can be raised within the culture, find employment within the industry, meet a companion with the same ideals, and never have to explore anything in life beyond these boundaries. So to my parents, teachers, and elders: never take for granted how powerful this rap industry and culture is. I have often heard KRS ONE say, " back in the day, your parents told you to get a degree just in case this rap thing doesn't work out, but now you need to learn how to rap, just in case your degree doesn't work out". How crazy is that?

So how do you tell a young urban mogul who rose from the bottomless pit of his community to accrue a net worth of 500 million to a billion dollars that his music and message has done the urban community more harm than good when all of the numbers and opportunities for advancement say otherwise? How do you tell a young generation who previously had no hope to earn an honest living who can now become entrepreneurs, or learn a valuable trade via editing, mixing, engineering, videography, and graphic designing that what they are doing is wrong and immoral? How do you tell a bunch of young thugs with criminal records who can barely read and write, yet have a unique skill set that can catapult them to the top of the world that their life is worthless? How do you tell a young woman with a beautiful body that she shouldn't exploit it to provide food, clothing, and shelter for her and her babies, where outside of the rap industry she has very few opportunities to survive? You don't. You simply attempt to view the situation through the eyes of the super oppressed and all of the opportunities that rap has afforded them. What other industry has provided more jobs and fulfilled more dreams for the poor? And if you cannot provide a viable option other than going to school to conform into the matrix of society to earn considerably less than what they could make in the rap industry, then there is absolutely nothing we can say to this generation, period. Even drug dealers are willing to trade in their hustle for a shot at fame and fortune, the blue print for them to do so has already been laid out by just about every successful rapper that has come before them. Drug dealers are now selling drugs with a purpose far greater than buying fancy cars, making it "rain" in the club, and popping champagne. Their ultimate goal now is to save enough money to one day get out of the streets, go legit, and become successful moguls. This is not just the blueprint laid out by today's rappers; it is also the blueprint of gangsters of all cultures with aspirations of making it in America.

The only problem is that most rappers cannot make the transition from the streets to the corporate boardrooms because they have not been properly educated in the fields of finance, economics, investments, etc. As a result, most of them who achieve fortune resort right back to what they know best, and that's buying fancy cars making it "rain" in the club, and popping champagne! However, there are a few who have cracked the code, and even though the corporate world can be just as vicious as the streets, the etiquette in which they operate by is just different. So these moguls had to change their hustle and approach, kudos to those who were able to make the adjustments. They have become assets to the corporate world. Meanwhile, these drug dealers/moguls in training are paying very close attention to the progress of their peers. In their eyes, their hustle is now validated by the results of a few moguls who were able to pull off the feat. In their eyes, selling drugs to their own people is justified if it means that they can successfully achieve their personal goals. Only in America can ones success be measured or predicated on someone else's demise. Unfortunately, we are quick to point out how drug dealers are killing their communities, but we fail to recognize that the pharmaceutical companies have set up shop on just about every corner doing the same exact thing, and they are both sanctioned by the government! Then there are your favorite celebrities who endorse soda products that have tons of sugar, which is just as addictive and harmful as illegal drugs. F.D.A. stand for food and drug administration. The only difference is that the food and drug administration and pharmaceutical companies don't make rap records bragging about supplying drugs to their own communities, they just cash their checks and keep it moving. This is the stark reality of the situation.

There is also a "Dark" side to the rap industry as well, an underworld so sinister that very few live to talk about it. No, I'm not talking about "Baphomet", the illuminati, or the satanic verbiage that has been running rampant in the industry lately. All of that has become the perfect distraction. I am talking about the underworld of organized crime. The rap industry is a multi billion-dollar enterprise. Whenever there is that much money being made and exchanged, there will be lots of drug trafficking, murder, and extortion. There is an entire subculture that operates out of the limelight, and this has been in operation long before rap was invented. The Italian mob, the Russian mob, and the Jewish mob have all claimed a stake in the music and movie industries for years. Now there is a new mob on the scene, the "Hood" mob. They may not be as organized but the still have a system in place to extort fake gangster rappers and industry big wigs that need protection from real criminals. This part of the subculture is usually made up of real hardened criminals with no chance of succeeding in life otherwise due to their extensive criminal records. The underworld provides millions of dollars for those bold enough to do the dirty work required to succeed, and most of them are just as ambitious as a rapper would be to make it. There is even a no fly zone that is implemented in certain cities. That means, when you touch down in one of these cities, you must immediately notify the hood that you are in town and pay the necessary "fees" to ensure a safe trip. It is important to understand just how many people the rap industry feeds, and get a better understanding of why there are those willing to kill to be a part of it.

The biggest feeders off of the rap industry are corporations. They sit at the top of the food pyramid. They hire young urban executives with an "eye" for talent to plug them into the life force of urban America. The rap industry has changed over the last ten years or so. Due to illegal downloads of music; the artist and the labels have suffered major losses, so a new revenue stream had to be created in order for the artist in particular to survive. That's where corporate America steps in. Many artists began signing endorsement deals to supplement their loss of royalties. It doesn't really matter what they are endorsing as long as they are being paid, most of them could care less of its residual effects on the consumer. So from soda to alcohol, from clothes to cars, it is clear to see that corporate America is in bed with urban America, and it is a very intimate relationship. Rap artist have become the ultimate conduit between the corporation and the consumers. If we trust the artist, we trust the product that they are selling us; it's that simple. If we no longer trust or are protesting against a particular artist, the advantage is with the corporation who can just shift their endorsement deal to the next artist that is urban approved. In some instances, having street credibility is a plus with corporations. It adds a sense of authenticity to the relationship. If we, the consumer truly feel an artist is living a certain lifestyle, we are more prone to believe that he or she uses the product that they are trying to pitch to us. Yet, in most cases, nothing could be further from the truth. Then there are the artists who endorse products from major corporations but do not get paid from it. Bentley doesn't have to advertise its cars because just about every rapper on the planet will do it for them!

Corporate America owns the rap industry, not the record labels. In fact, the labels are just benefactors of the relationship between its artists and the corporations. There use to be a time when artist could survive off of touring, selling merchandise, etc. This money went directly to the artist. Unfortunately, now the labels have forced them to sign these new 360 deals where they (label) get a percentage of everything related to the career of that artist, and I mean everything! Since corporate America are the ones writing the checks, they are the ones calling all of the shots. This creates a major problem. The relationship between the artist and the corporation renders the rapper useless when it comes to critical issues that need to be address regarding social events like police brutality, discrimination, and violence. Rappers cannot speak freely for fear of losing their endorsements. So they have essentially become slaves to the corporations. This is the difference between Hip Hop and rap. In the beginning, Hip Hop gave a voice to the voiceless; it fought for the people so it only had to answer to the people. The corporations' own rap so it has the final say on what its employees can address or what they must steer clear of. In this sense, rap is anti Hip Hop.

The culture of rap has become the "dream catcher". Once inside of its notorious web it becomes hard for many young African-American men and women to escape. Their dreams begin and end in the pursuit of fame and fortune. The journey to reach such an illusive goal can become very taxing on the mind, body, and soul. Very few make it, and those that do are a mere shell of themselves with nothing to truly show for it besides a few material possessions, newspaper clippings, and a story to tell their grandchildren in the future. The majority of others who do not make it provide the necessary energy to create a profitable industry where everything related to the industry are for sale. Let's face it; pursuing your dreams cost money, so drum machines, keyboards, editing software, cameras, managers, photographers and auditions fuel the economic base of the industry. It's no different then if your dream was to become a basketball player. Sneakers, basketballs, head bands, and camps eat up your finances, while the time, energy, and sacrifice required to become a part of the 1% that actually make it eats up your dream. This capitalist system is set up to feed off of and control your destiny whether you succeed or not. As a result of this process, I have witnessed many artists devote their entire being to the exhausting chase of a record deal under the guise that their music will change the landscape of the industry. And it doesn't matter if they are conscious rappers or hardcore gangster rappers; the notion is the same.

I have seen artist abandon their children, wives, jobs, and lifestyle over a thirty-year period with nothing to show for it but the new demo in their pocket that is sure to be the one that gets them signed this time around. A 40 year old rapper with a demo or mix tape in hip pocket, who is behind on his child support payments, living off of the means of women that they can take advantage of, while standing on the corner smoking weed all day is pathetic! Yeah, I said it. And even though they know in their heart of hearts that the rap industry is poison, they are now trapped in the dream catcher's web because they have not learned a skill beyond rap in any capacity. Now there is a new generation of twelve year olds who are about to repeat the same cycle. From an urban standpoint it has become very frustrating to watch an entire movement of people pigeonhole their dreams into rap or rap related industries, which is heavily overpopulated. Meanwhile, the opportunities for growth in the fields of science, engineering, architecture, and business are understaffed because not enough people are qualified to fill these positions. And the urban communities contribution to these fields are almost non-existent. Yet these are the fields that literally change the world, but we continue to reduce ourselves to entertaining the world. To suggest that this is all that we are great at negates our great history of being mathematicians, scientists, and builders who gave the current world its foundation to stand on.

Yes, the rap industry is a multi billion-dollar industry these days, but the culture vultures are the ones who have benefited the most. When all of the smoke is clear, we receive a mere fraction of the proceeds generated from the very talent that we, and only we possess. So just as all of the other cultures or subcultures that I have previously explained in this chapter, the underlining motive is the same, economics. However, this faction doesn't have anything to do with an outside ethnic group or race of people, it is based on a capitalist group. The music industry is a unique one in the sense that is strictly built on the talent of its artist, yet the artists receive the least amount of dividends for their service. However, this is not a how-to book about the rap industry, or how to make it in the music business. Yet the rap industry is one of the many components that make up urban culture as a whole. In order to understand todays' youth, we must at least try to understand their mindset and approach to making it out of the hood and the realistic options they have for accomplishing that goal. Where those outside of the urban community see violence, sex, drugs, misogyny, homophobia and the likes; those within the urban community see opportunity, wealth, fame, and a very bright future. And they are both correct, so perspective is everything in this case.

One last point that I feel needs to be made when talking about the culture of the rap industry; it is a dying industry! "World music" is on the rise and will soon take over the industry as the leading moneymaker. This is critical because world music consist of all of the genres of music with a universal 4/4 beat. It can be a little Hip Hop, a little bit of R&B, a little bit of rock music, a little bit of heavy metal, etc. rap has been gradually minimized over the last 5 years or so. Most of the lyrics of world music are about love, partying and having a great time as opposed to the lyrics of current rap songs, which continue to focus on sex, drugs, and gunplay. It's almost like placing a dirty glass next to a clean one. Just as the title states, world music is worldwide. And since music in general is universal, one can only wonder if this new one world music could become the precursor for a one-world religion, or a one-world government. Those who have dedicated their lives to rap as opposed to the culture of Hip Hop may be finished in the next couple of years. This world music also has the potential to redefine the word urban. It may now extend beyond the boundaries of just the city lines. It may truly be more of a lifestyle no matter where you live, or what your race, color or creed is. Now let's move on...

Now that we have meticulously deciphered a vast amount of information regarding the residual effects of urban culture, let's not lose sight of what gave birth to this current cultural paradigm in the first place, Hip Hop. When the true history of this generation is written it will begin and end with the emergence of Hip Hop the art form, not rap which is the commercialized, bastardized version of it, not twerking which is the sexualized, perverted aspect of it, not drug selling and violence which is the over-glamorized portion of it, but the art form itself. And make no mistake about it; Hip Hop is an art form. It's made up of all of the characteristics of every other art form, just urbanized! To all of the naysayers who refuse to see it as a legitimate art form, it really doesn't matter what you think personally because millions around the world do see it as an art form and practice it as such everyday. It has become their religion. It has become their way of life. It has become their culture. Hip Hop is the language of the commoners and if you do not speak their language, then you are an alien to their cause, to their struggle, and to their well being. Yet in order for Hip Hop to really flourish, the artistic value of it must be restored, because the way to ascension from the earthly realm is through art. Even most religious buffs would have to agree that it is through praising the most high using song, dance, reciting spiritual passages, sacred pictures, and mythological stories that enhances their religious experiences. And this ultimately brings them closer to the most high. So let us always respect and honor the true essence of art.

CHAPTER 21

ART'S AFFECT ON SOCIETY AND SOCIETY'S AFFECT ON ART

Over the years art has been known to imitate life. It is the spiritual pulse of a people. Art is the gateway used to make the unseen seen, or the unheard heard. It is true magic and the artists who have perfected their craft are some of the greatest magicians that the world has ever known. They are heavily revered for their ability to transform the world into a better place. So ultimately, it is art the gives shape to a society. This is why in ancient times art was held in such high regards. Any society that is art deficient is probably one filled with crime, unemployment and overall stagnation because there is no art to inspire. This was the exact state of urban America before the birth of Hip Hop. And Hip Hop is unique because being deprived of art in the traditional sense is what gave birth to it in the first place. Now, there will be many doubters who will state that many urban communities are still infested with crime, drugs, and unemployment, even after the arrival of Hip Hop. But let's examine Hip Hop in its infancy and see how it raised the energy of inner city youth, as well as the positive affect that it had on our society as a whole before it was coopted and corrupted by the greed of corporations. Let us place some of the conspirators on trial before we pass judgment. When art is allowed to flow freely like water in a stream or river, it continually refreshes and renews itself. But when it become stagnant, it becomes polluted like a filthy pond. Herein lays the answer as to what happened to Hip Hop. Societies affect on the artistic nature of Hip Hop caused the initial stagnation. Allow me to explain. Many movie directors, musicians, and artist alike draw inspiration from their immediate surroundings or life experiences.

The more an artist is in touch with his or her community, and can use their particular muse to convey this artistically will ultimately determine how many people can relate to their works. This is why the average kid from the hood can relate to Rappers, Hustlers and Ballers. Because they come from the same upbringing and have found a way to defy the odds and make it in today's society. Where we come from rapping, hustling and "ballin" is an art form. The advent of the Internet, reality shows and music videos has given maximum exposure to what was once delegated to the streets of urban America. From Hollywood to corporate America, there is no denying that Hip Hop has had a tremendous affect on our society. Some Hip Hop enthusiast might think that's great, but in doing so it has created, what I like to call an "echo" affect where art is no longer imitating life, but life is now imitating art! It seems like every commercial, movie, magazine, and even sports network is using Hip Hop to sell or convey messages aimed at our youth. When we look at this through the eyes of an inner city child who is easily impressionable, this has a great affect on how they perceive life, what they want to be when they grow up, and even how they go about creating their art. What they think is an original thought is most likely one that has been implanted by the television, the Internet, or other forms of media. That's a reflection of art that has been ping ponged back and forth so many times that it's hard to determine the original source. So instead of our art influencing the world, the world, in the form of its media outlets can actually use our art as a form of control. If the artistic expression of a people is not allowed to flow freely, then its people are not free.

Ask any child from the inner city what they would like to become when they grow up, and most of them will say rappers, hustlers and ballers. Not because that is an original thought, but because that's what society has painted as the picture of success for them. So they no longer try to break the mold by thinking outside of the box, but further secure the mold by staying within the parameters set up by someone else's perception of them artistically. Hip Hop has had a profound affect on our society. The art, fashion, music, and overall culture have given a voice to a people who would be unheard otherwise. It has also made a lot of people rich. Not just the artist themselves, but it has been the best thing to happen to Hollywood and corporate America in a very long time. Remember, Hip Hop is worldwide, so its sphere of influence has no limitations. Yet society has had a profound affect on Hip Hop as well. It has shut down the artistic channels by making it so commercial that it can't move forward to raise the vibration of the people who need it the most, our youth. It has taken the worst aspects of Hip Hop (rap), and made it the most financially rewarding. Sex and violence sells, but artistically it kills because it has an influence in the creative process of the next generation of artists. They don't create to change the world; they create to reap the financial benefits that the world has to offer. Art, fame and money don't necessarily go together.

The God within us must create or it dies. This is how we live forever. Art is forever; money and fame will come and go. There are those who are fortunate enough to receive all three, and that's great. But as parents, teachers and elders alike, we want to challenge our youth to follow their hearts and find inspiration beyond the norm, and not be afraid to express an original thought, and allow the fame and money to be an aftermath of this process. We want our youth to influence the world in a positive manner. This will bring about real change. We don't want the negative aspects of the world to influence our youth. That will create a never-ending cycle of destruction. Our fight is with the many exterior forces that bombard our children's psyche every day, and that's any and every media outlet that resonates with a message other than love, or one of a positive nature. We can't force them to turn off the television, log off of the Internet, or ignore the many billboard ads that promote someone else's agenda. These media streams are here forever, but we can make them aware of the interior forces that lay dormant within them that, when activated can serve as protection against anything negative that may try to invade their space. And that's knowledge of self. Hip Hop has had a great affect on society, not all good and not all bad. Society has to take some responsibility for allowing the lower aspects of the culture (rap) to grow out of control for the sake of entertainment and profits. We as parents and teachers also have to take responsibility for the direction that our youth are heading in. We have to embrace Hip Hop; don't fight it. Spend time learning about the culture and how to use it to your advantage and the people that you are trying to reach will become more of an alley than an enemy.

CHAPTER 22

THE CULTURE OF URBAN EDUCATION

Why doesn't the educational system work in this country? Is it because the curriculum hasn't really changed in the last 60 years? Is it because teachers are using old school methods in a new school society? What about the classroom structure? How about the teacher to student ratio? Are African-American children's brains hardwired differently than European children's? All of these are valid questions that I will attempt to address. I believe it was Albert Einstein who said, "Doing the same things and expecting different results is insanity." How many times have we said, "these children today are crazy" without giving much thought to the process that may have contributed to their insanity? Our children are not the same children that we were growing up. They were not raised under the same circumstances, conditions or moral standards. They were birthed in a different day and time, a time of greater challenges, greater hardships, as well as greater responsibilities. The technology and overall knowledge on the planet has also increased tenfold, which means their consciousness has also increased. Once the consciousness expands, so should the educational methods used to teach our youth as well. When it doesn't it creates a major problem because the synchronicity of mind, body, and soul are off.

The mind, body and soul should be in accord at all times. If the mind is stagnant, due to an educational system that is not relevant for this day and time, it will eventually manifest in the form of disinterest, dropout rates, failure, etc. If the body is not supplied with the proper nourishment that enhances one's ability to learn on a higher level, then our youth will continue to be sluggish; which will result in lower energy outputs. And finally, the soul, which is usually left out of the equation when it comes to education, must be addressed if we are to begin to educate the next generation holistically. Our youth are having amazing spiritual awakenings that no one has prepared them for so they suppress these experiences for fear of being ridiculed or scrutinized. I'm not talking about religion; I'm talking about spirituality. Religion is a roadmap that can be used to guide us on our spiritual journey if we ever lose our way. Spirituality supersedes all religions because it is innate. Religion is a choice, and there are many great ones to choose from. Spirituality is your birthright. I know that religion in school is a touchy subject, but teaching the universal language of spirituality doesn't threaten one's religious beliefs. If anything, it enhances it. If our children are taught that they are spiritual beings having a human experience, it changes their perception of reality exponentially. Until these issues are addressed, our children will be completely out of sync. The education system should renew itself every three years or so. What is true today may not necessarily be true tomorrow.

All textbooks should be destroyed because at the rate that we are making new discoveries, by the time the information is printed, most of it is probably obsolete. Textbooks seem to etch things in stone in the minds of our youth. For instance, our children should not still be learning that Christopher Columbus discovered America when we now know and can prove that the only thing he discovered was that he was lost. This also reinforces white superiority on a subconscious level by suggesting that you can discover a landmass that is already occupied. In the case of African Americans, they are only taught about their arrival in Jamestown Virginia in the year of 1619 as slaves and savages, when in fact, they have a very rich history here as Moors, as well as on the other side of the Atlantic Ocean that if they were educated about would most certainly infuse a sense of pride far greater than that of a slave. So instead of having the mentality of a slave of savage, they can have the mentality of a King or Queen. This also does a disservice to white students as well because they feel that everyone else is invading their land when in fact most of us arrived on ships, either as slaves or free men, and everyone has an equal right to the land.

A lot of times, the teachers do not reflect the community that they are teaching in. This is critical because if the children feel that you cannot relate to them or vise versa, they shut down. Most children from the inner city do not come to school with an open mind. They are not an open canvass ready to be painted on. Their minds are bogged down with so much stress due to life circumstances that an education is the furthest from their minds. Crime, poverty, abuse, and violence are real issues that are all too common for them. School becomes a safe haven of sorts to escape the real hardships faced by today's youth. Children can also feel the love and concern from their teachers. When they feel that someone really cares about them, they tend to work harder because they don't want to let them down. This is a critical component to teaching in the inner cities because a lot of our children don't get that love and attention at home, so when they show up at school it's not necessarily for an education per se. They are seeking to have a void filled. And when it is, they feel they have a sense of purpose, and when young bright minds have a sense of purpose, the sky is the limit. But when they sense that the teacher is just there to get a paycheck, they act out and rebel. Role models generally have better success because they are usually from the same upbringing and can relate to the struggles face by today's youth. But they usually only satisfy one half of the equation which are the domestic challenges faced. Holistically educating our children is the greatest challenge, especially for European teachers who are accustomed to teaching in a more linear fashion. Our dance, fashion, art, and other family traditions are tools for learning. If we can't place ourselves into a situation or associate with a story being told, we lose interest. We need to be able to use a balance of our left and right brain when it comes to learning. Our left side is our logical side and our right side is our creative side. A creative story masked within a logical moral lesson would probably work wonders.

The rap industry has played a significant role in the dropout rate as well. Why go to school to acquire an education to earn forty, maybe fifty thousand a year, when you can sit at home and write rhymes or produce beats and make ten times that amount? The rap industry has created an "out" for inner city youth who are academically challenged to begin with. It becomes almost impossible to convince a child of the importance of an education when most of the rap artist are high school dropouts who make millions promoting the very opposite of what society considers a progressive lifestyle. We cannot negate the impact that music videos, movies, and the attention that sports figures receive. They have a great influence on the minds of our youth. Everyday our children are being bombarded with images, sounds, and the overall lifestyle of athletes, hustlers, rappers, video vixens, etc. What teacher can compete with that? We live in a microwave world where everyone wants instant and tangible results. So going to college or high school for that matter for four years will not fill the immediate needs of a young man or woman fascinated with the material lifestyle of their favorite artist or Hollywood idol. They want it and they want it now, so they will be willing to go on a reality show, sell drugs, become a stripper, or pimp to get it. The old traditional way of thinking from our parents of going to school, working hard, getting a good job and retiring is "played out". What's ironic is that most of the people at the very top of the pyramid in the movie and music industry all have degrees of higher learning. This should be a lesson onto itself. I am in no way suggesting that our youth shouldn't create music or make movies, but truly owning the rights to ones intellectual property requires certain levels of smarts which can only come from being properly educated in these fields. Just try reading the standard music contract given to each new artist. So we as parents, teachers and elders are in a war with those who can produce what appear to be instant tangible results. But these results have no true substance other than the illusion of success. Success should be defined on an individual bases and may have nothing to do with money at all. Our youth are so caught up in the destination, when the true lessons are learned on the journey of life itself.

A lot of the education system today is based on memory. If you can memorize the lessons being taught and regurgitate it back on the test, then you can succeed in the current school system structure. But is this the proper way to educate, or is this the proper way to program? Let's examine the concept. From an early age our children are uploaded with tons of information on many subjects, math, science, history, etc. Then they are tested to see how well they remember the information previously given. Beyond the math and reading, most of the information is deleted right after the test because it is not applicable to the child's life, or it doesn't serve the immediate needs of the child. Not many will agree, but most of the subjects taught in grade school and beyond serve no purpose but to occupy a child's mind with things that are irrelevant to their overall growth and productivity. I am not saying that these subjects are not important; I am saying that the way that they are taught to us is wrong. It's one thing to memorize a science formula, and it's something totally different to take apart, analyze, decipher, and find the connection between you and the formula itself, the latter forces one to think as opposed to just memorize. Our teachers have to begin to show them the connection between everything in life, using a holistic approach to each and every subject. Our perception is based on the information that is imputed in our database. The disinterest in school can be attributed to the outdated information being uploaded, when our children have already received "upgraded" processors.

Let's encourage critical thinking and allow our children to explore all of the possibilities before they arrive at a conclusion. The memory form of "learning" creates drones, which just follow orders. This is mind control at its best. Who does this type of education really benefit? Do not underestimate a child's ability to subconsciously rebel against the system that is trying to turn them into robots. Most teachers have a curriculum that they must follow. But they must challenge themselves to come outside of that box and really prepare their children for the future. If not, then they are only doing the child as well as themselves a disservice in the long run.

The new common core curriculum now being implemented across the country is an attempt to rewire the way our children think. It forces them to go through a series of monotonous steps to find the answer to an equation, or to perform a psychoanalysis on what an author was thinking when they wrote a passage. This concept may work well with children of European decent. Their thought process seems to resonate more on a logical, linear pattern. So following a step-by-step formula makes all of the sense in the world to them. Children of African descent are hardwired differently. They think more in creative wavelengths or outside of the box. Now, let me state that neither way of thinking is wrong, just different. A creative thinker is trying to find the quickest way to the answer, if he or she can arrive at the same results without going through all of the steps, then they are satisfied. For instance, if the math problem is 250x20 why not just remove the zeros then multiply 25x2 which is much easier to figure out, then add the two zeros back at the end to get your answer? Or if you are adding 37+48 why not just round both numbers to the nearest ten, then subtract 3 and 2 to arrive at your answer? That's one of the ways African children view numbers, but this method is no longer accepted. They don't just want the answer; they want to know how you arrived at that particular answer or you only receive partial credit. Most of the time, they can't even tell you how they came up with an answer; they just know that it is right.

Children of African descent know that numbers, letters, and nature are just external expressions of their internal being. Our ancestors had a saying, "I am that I am" so how I arrived to this point, or came up with a particular answer in the rudimentary sense is irrelevant. These are some of the holistic principles that need to be taught to children of African descent who attend public schools, but are not. Children of Urban America suffer and become stagnant in their ability to filter through the many processes and steps required when it comes to understanding math and science in this country. As a result, they become bored with it and do not fair well on state tests. So our low scores are not a true assessment of our ability to understand math and science, but rather our inability to grasp the European methods in which it is being taught to our children.

CHAPTER 23

THE CULTURE OF SEX

This subject has become taboo for most parents yet it is the most talked about topic between children. Children now have access to information regarding sex that we as adults didn't have ten, fifteen years ago. The Internet has opened "Pandora's box," filled with visuals, sound effects, and vivid instructions on how to participate. Long gone are the days when a teen would come across a dirty magazine and his or her curiosity could only fill in some of the blanks. We as parents are at the mercy of what I call cyber child molesters and cyber perverts, who feed off of the curiosity of young children. They are lurking around every cyber corner, waiting for an opportunity to expose them with pop ups, deceiving adds, and other tricks like misspelled addresses. For instance, if a child misspells Disney.com, they can easily get a made up address that's spelled similar, like "Dicme.com" or something similar that is purposely spelled a certain way to take advantage of unsuspecting children. Activating a child's sexual energy prematurely is extremely dangerous, and once it's turned on rarely is it turned off. Conversations regarding sex are usually reserved for teenagers, but with all of the music videos and TV shows that are laced with sexual innuendo, its imperative that parents embrace a bold concept of talking to their pre teens about sex.

Our children are exposed to more about sex than we would like to admit, so we can choose to ignore the elephant in the room, or address it, and even more important than the act of sex itself, it the aspect of love and relationship as it pertains to sex. We always seem to gloss over that portion of relationship and go straight to the act itself. In doing so, we never fully teach them about the true purpose of sex. So most teen's get a crash course primarily focused on the physical act and most of them never recover, and the conversation should be the same for boy and girls. This male driven society has young boys – particularly those of African American descent – thinking that it is ok to have all of the sex that they desire without the need for love and understanding. This is what has contributed to all of the sexual assaults on women. Most of their favorite rappers are adding to the confusion because they actually have wives at home that they love, but their music reflects a life of extreme womanizing. The urban community is strife with broken, or single parent homes so the very concept of love and understanding is complex at the very least to grasp. Sex is complicated, but here are just a few of the things that must be addressed regarding it.

Sexual Magnetism

We all have a magnetic energy about us. Our thoughts are things that attract, usually things of the same nature. We have all heard the term "think positive" and by thinking positive, we are attempting to draw positive energy our way. But when we apply this concept to other aspects of life, the same rules apply. If we think negative, then most likely we will draw negative results. So when we think sexual, the end result will be of a sexual nature. There are other critical factors regarding the results of this science, like how much energy is focused towards a specific goal, as well as external triggers that keep you thinking about that specific goal. This will ultimately determine the rate of speed in which your results are achieved. This is why billions of dollars are spent every year on billboards and other forms of advertisements, because they work. When you see a commercial X number of times, you are eventually drawn to that particular product, or the chances of you choosing that product over another one are heavily increased. Sexual magnetism works the same way. Children are drawn to that which they are exposed to. Just turn on the television or listen to the radio and you will get a general idea of what's on their minds. The science of magnetism works with willing or unwilling participants. Consciously you may not be thinking about sex, but on a deeper, subconscious level, we can still be taken advantage of. In fact, it has been proven that the subconscious energy is much stronger than what we think on the surface.

Children will naturally become curious about sex, but thinking about sex in a curious or even casual sense, and being consumed are two different things altogether. You can monitor you child's sexual magnetism by watching the way they dress, talk, their musical preference, etc. At times age is not a factor. There are nine-year-old girls who exude the sexual energy of grown women and adult men are easily drawn to them and the results can be tragic. Especially if the adult male is weak minded and has the mentality of a child, and then magnetically, it is a perfect fit. This is one of the many reasons why perverts and molesters are drawn to children. Be aware of the sexual triggers that activate your child's curiosity like; what they watch on the internet, their interest in boys, TV programs of a subtle sexual nature, sexting on their cell phones, etc. Daydreaming, especially for girls, is another sign of sexual magnetism.

Bi-Curious

There is a new trend among teenagers and even some pre teens. The term bi-curious is used to describe their curiosity about sex with the same gender. There are no more boundaries when it comes to teenage love, lust, or sex. This can be dangerous because before they can even learn the basic principles of something as complicated as sex, they are already delving into advanced situations, most of the time this leaves the child confused after such experience dissipates. This usually leads to more empty relationships, filled with even greater sexual exploitations. Let's not forget the emotional trauma of such experience as well. In the past, exposure to such lifestyles was extremely limited due to the way this type of behavior was looked upon. So it would be years before parents were able to learn of their children's sexual preference. But today's society is much more open-minded regarding this subject, and in most cases the children aren't hiding so the dialogue between parent and child can be an open honest one. The bi-curious stage is usually a passing fad, or a form of rebellion against what is considered normal or in some cases, just to piss their parents off.

Tri-Sexual

Once this sexual energy is activated and the bi-curious stage has subsided, normal sex seems outdated. So the next phase is tri-sexual, which means that they will "try" anything to satisfy their sexual appetite. This includes but is not limited to multiple partners, orgies, sex toys, S&M, etc. what they perceive as sexual freedom is usually an emotional nightmare. They have not yet learned of the emotional and spiritual connection to sex. We as parents have not taught this to them because most of us haven't experienced it ourselves. Or we have simply underestimated the importance of teaching it to our children. So there sexual experiences are void of any true meaning beyond a physical release. This is significant because their every day relationships become cold and callas. They become emotionally detached and isolated. Teachers will usually see a drop in attendance as well as in an interest in schoolwork. The children may even become violent at times. A child's very first sexual experience is critical. If it's a female and she is having unprotected sex with a male, she receives his energy into her in the form of semen. His semen carries his programming. If he is abusive, uncaring, unintelligent, etc. then she will undoubtedly be persuaded by his energy, and since it's the first time having sex, in most cases this energy will never leave her. I don't care how many relationships she has after that. The same thing applies to gay men. The giver usually programs the receiver. This is generally affective when there is an exchange of fluids but is in no way limited to just that. Sex opens you up psychically as well, so during orgasms, energy is also exchanged. This process is genderless.

Psychic Sex

Psychic sex is usually reserved for those who are looking to dominate their victim not only physically, but also mentally and psychologically as well. A child's brain that isn't fully developed becomes the perfect candidate for such perverse behavior. The traumatizing process of being sexually violated over and over again can force certain children to create altered egos to escape the physical pain that they are forced to endure. In other words, they "travel" to a far way place deep within their subconscious mind to escape the pain, yet when doing so, they are usually being instructed by the abuser with specific orders to be carried out later, or to only remember what the abuser wants them to remember. The children almost become robotic in nature, or soulless. Psychic sex is usually performed during these elaborate sex rituals, which takes place in a lot of these underground cults. In most cases children are used because a "virgin" is needed to sacrifice to whatever entity that they are trying to appease. In the case of a boy, if he has not been anally violated, he is equivalent to being a virgin. Most of us do not believe that these types of atrocities against children are humanly possible, or if we do believe that it is possible, we think that it is only happening in some rural town mile way from the urban community. Yet consider this, thousands of children are reported missing from the hood every year. Some of this can be attributed to runaways, or organ harvesting, but a lot of it can also be attributed to sexual predators of all natures.

Sexually Active Virgins

There is a new wave of sexual activity among teens that involves oral and anal sex without vaginal penetration. Technically, they are still virgins according to the definition of such. This allows them to still participate in sexual activity under the pretense of being a virgin. So for those parents who take their children to the doctor to verify that they are still virgins, now they have to test for anal penetration as well. The sexual climate in school these days is so strong that young girls in particular are put under so much stress and peer pressure, that they are forced into uncompromising positions in order to compete for the affection of boys. So they compromise their sexual integrity by offering oral and or anal sex to satisfy the sexual desires of horny little boys, all the while keeping their promise to their parents to save themselves for when they get older. This can be dangerous for numerous reasons, including the exchange of bodily fluids, the physical damage that it can cause, as well as the psychological damage it can caused.

Masturbation

This is usually the very first sexual experience that a child will have. It generally starts around the age of 11 or 12. However, it can start as early as six or seven years old. The natural curiosity to explore ones body comes with a price. Exhaustion, mental fatigue, and the overall loss of energy are just some of the symptoms of chronic masturbation. The power of an orgasm is far greater than we have been taught to believe. It is a mini explosion of great proportion. It is atomic in nature and affects everything in your personal environment. It heightens the magnetism of thought. So whatever you are thinking, consciously or subconsciously at the time of an orgasm is being "birthed" on some level or another. This is called Sex magic in many occult or esoteric circles. Before we as parents or teachers dismiss this as just some "new age" mumbo jumbo, do the research on the validity of such practices. The skin parties that are all the rave in Europe and that are now making their way to the United States are deeply rooted in Sex Magic.

Masturbation creates anti-social beings as well. Children and adults alike practice the self-satisfying process of sexual arousal. The loss of vital proteins and minerals due to ejaculation begin to tax the body heavily. Our sex organs represent creativity. This is how man and woman bring (create) life into a physical existence. So every time that we ejaculate or reach an orgasm for pleasure without the proper understanding of sexual energy, we lose our creative essence. The more we do it, the weaker we become creatively speaking. So sitting at home masturbating creates a form of mental stasis. This is critical for the development of young minds. Our environment is sexually polluted with our thoughts, as well as the "invisible" energy that we release every time we reach an orgasm. There are devices used by crime scene investigators to detect semen left by potential suspects of sexual crimes. It is of an infrared nature that cannot be detected by the naked eye, but this is only half the story. Every orgasm reached, either by masturbation or otherwise has an "etheric" energy released that is also invisible to the naked eye. Science has made great strides in the last few years, creating devices that can see the full spectrum of our auras, and one day our entire medical, sexual, and biological energy fields will be seen by all. But until that time parents must use the obvious signs to determine if their child suffers from chronic masturbation, as well as common ways to combat it.

Urban Sexual Warfare

What happens when the victim now becomes the abuser? We have more victims, and this begins the never-ending cycle of abuse of innocent children hood-wide. The mentally of "it happened to me, so I will take it out on you" has ruined many lives before they even truly get started. Children in urban areas are easy prey. Most of them are basically taking care of themselves on a daily basis to begin with. Couple that with the prison culture that no one ever seems to want to talk about, and we have the perfect breeding ground for this type of sick behavior. After being violated, a lot of our children grow up confused as to what their sexual orientation is. There are even some men who do not consider themselves to be gay, but only sleep with other men or young boys. Yet the biggest rise in this behavior is with young women. Women are turning out other young women at an alarming rate. However, because most of us are trained to watch the actions of men, they are able to operate under the radar so to speak. Nowadays, you have to watch everybody. Trust no one around your children. Be careful of just letting them spend a night a friend's house that may have a brother, uncle or even an aunt who is a predator. Remember, it only takes a few minutes to destroy a child's life forever. I truly believe that these types of violations of our children is one of the main reasons why they are so violent, on drugs, sexually confused, unable to learn, or unable to fit in socially.

Sex Sells…Movies, Music, and Products

It also sells our children's souls down the drain with false promises of success that can be attained by simply showing their bodies in a sexual manner. Pre-teen and teenagers alike heavily watch rap videos and most of them have something relating to sex in them. Long gone are the days of creative videos that deal with a full rage of issues that affect our community. It's so blatant today that the lyrics from the songs are not even in synchronicity with the video, meaning, the lyrics don't have to be of a sexual nature, they can be violent, but the images shown will still be about sex. This type of cross-synchronicity becomes a valuable marketing tool that can be used to sell anything because it can be cleverly linked back to sex. This also desensitizes our children when it comes to sex. This is why we have a very high rate of young women who are willing to become strippers or even sell their bodies for next to nothing. There is no emotion attached to the act of sex anymore, its just business, and this is also why young men have absolutely no respect for women.

The rap industry has created a market for women with big booties and extra large breasts. Some of the women are even willing to go to the extreme of getting plastic surgery to enhance these features, the greater the enhancement, the greater the opportunity to turn these artificial features into a lucrative career as a video vixen. The movie industry is no different as it uses certain images to define what beauty is. All of the teen movies deal with "love" and relationships and focus on outer beauty, placing extreme pressure on young women in particular to maintain a certain lifestyle. The beauty product industry thrives off of our low self esteem as well. A brand new industry of artificial parts and limbs is amongst us, where any and all body parts can be replaced until satisfaction is reached. The men in videos are always surrounded by more women than they can handle to give off the impression of great sexual prowess, meanwhile their pouring champagne all over them, calling them out of their names, and even raising the status of other men above women. This further degrades them as if they are not even human. Some say that this type of behavior stems from slave times when slave masters would encourage such promiscuous behavior from Black men for the sole purpose of breeding more productive slaves. The duty of a very strong and productive male slave would be to impregnate as many female slaves as possible as to ensure a greater stock of future slaves.

This process had absolutely nothing to do with love; it simply focused on the physical act itself. If this is the case, then this sexual behavior is embedded deep within the subconscious mind of black Men, and may even go as deep as within the DNA structure. Then there are those who say it goes even further than that. At the height of our reign in ancient Khemet (Africa), men could have as many wives as they could afford to take care of. If this were the case, then this too would have a direct affect on the DNA of a young black man. The more that things change; the more they remain the same. This attitude has become a part of the culture of young inner city men and women. And the movie and music industry packages, promotes, and then sells this same culture right back to our young. And they buy it hook, line, and sinker.

CHAPTER 24

THE CULTURE OF DRUG USE

T he United States makes up about 16 percent of the worlds population, but makes up about 93 percent of the worlds drug users, and this does not include alcohol, caffeine, or tobacco! Drug use is embedded in the very fiber of American culture. Our youth and their drug behavior is a direct byproduct of this culture. What is a child's fascination or curiosity with experiencing an altered state of mind, or escaping a certain reality? Is it programming, peer pressure, or a rite of passage? It may be all of the above. And this is critical for parents and teachers to understand, if we are to combat the problem at its core.

Drugs and DNA

When I speak of programming, I mean this in the literal sense of one's DNA. The technical term is deoxyribonucleic acid, which is a macromolecule responsible for the transference of genetic characteristics in all life forms. In other words, it stores the genetic codes to who you are. These codes are passed down from generation to generation. This is why if you are diagnosed with cancer, the doctor will ask you; is there a history of cancer in your family? So if your parents or parent's parents were heavy drug abusers, you may be susceptible to such vices from a molecular standpoint. The code which triggers this abuse can be anything from a certain food, event, thought, etc. But these codes can be changed or reprogrammed with the proper knowledge of self, diet and thought process. The 80's and 90's was commonly called the crack era in many urban neighborhoods. As crack flooded the streets of many homes, it subsequently flooded the thought stream and blood stream of many young men and women who began to abandon their children on street corners just for a five dollar hit. They were selling their bodies, murdering innocent people, and wreaking havoc on their own communities. Many children were birthed, not out of the energy of love, but in a chaotic state of prostitution, violence, duress, desperation, anger, resentment, etc. It seemed like a generation of soulless children were born. Our great ancestors had a saying, "all is mental". If this is the case, then sperm could be considered as the physical representation of a man's thoughts. So if his mind is ravished by crack, or his every thought is consumed by crack, or if crack is in his bloodstream, then he will undoubtedly transfer that energy to the unborn child in some capacity. Remember, as I just mentioned in the previous chapter, the male imprints the female because he is the giver so to speak and she is the receiver. This does not suggest in any way that the female is not responsible for the mental, physical, or spiritual outcome of the child.

Each parent contributes 23 chromosomes to the process of creation. So the mothers thought process or physical essence has a great affect on the child's well being. What she eats enters the child via the blood stream. What she thinks can also secrete a chemical reaction that enters the blood stream. This is in no way limited to crack. The same thing applies to alcohol, tobacco, pills, etc. But crack in particular really changed the DNA of an entire generation almost overnight. Tobacco and alcohol have been around so long that our DNA, which is ever changing has adjusted to accommodate for the use of such vices to some degree, and the same has happened with crack over time. It is not as potent as it was twenty-five years ago. However, the generation most affected by the crack epidemic is now in their late twenties or early thirties. So we as a community are just beginning to feel the true after-effects of the imprinting of an entire generation. The fact that they are more prone to violence, extreme sexual behavior, and drugs is directly related to the use and abuse of crack cocaine by their parents. I challenge anyone to refute this. The mental properties afforded most people who were born drug free have somehow escaped this generation. They are not as sensitive to the human condition or plight as generations' prior. They are also very materialistic. I believe that this is also linked to the fact that money or objects of value were needed to purchase crack, so money and material objects became synonymous with crack. As a result, this is what consumed the minds of many during this era, creating a collective mind-set or what some have called group think. This also includes the crack dealer, whose wealth grew exponentially as a result of crack consuming their every thought as well. They just operated from the other side of the spectrum. But let's not forget that they were making babies too. So they too are responsible for this generation of youth who put a greater value on materialistic things than anything else.

The word community when broken down is common unity, so no one involved with crack in any capacity can say that they were immune to the after-affects that we see today. You can hear and see the results of such materialist mindsets in today's music and music videos. Case in point, the urban generation born in the sixties had more of a revolutionary mindset because the focus of their parents at the time were rooted in civil rights, discrimination, police brutality, etc. So the Hip Hop movement of the eighties was mostly revolutionary. These were the teens of that day. So the tree is responsible for the fruit that it bares. As the saying goes, "the apple doesn't fall too far from the tree." In order to understand what the future holds as far as our youth are concerned, we need to pay close attention to the types of drugs that are being used by this generation. While it won't paint the entire picture, it will at least give us a snapshot of what we are up against. Today's drugs of choice are codeine mixed with cough syrup, methamphetamines. There are also exotic blends of marijuana, OxyContin, sherm, ecstasy (molly), and some college kids are even experimenting with inhaling human feces! So you do the math on where our youth are heading. Our DNA will play a major role in recording these events and becoming the blueprint for generations to come. We are all victims of programming. The question then becomes; is the programming internal (DNA) or from an external source (mind control) or both.

Drugs and Mind Control

Now that we have covered drugs from an internal point of view, we must examine the exterior influences that our youth face. Add placement has come a long way since the days of movie stars smoking cigarettes as a sign of being cool or as a part of their status. Warp speed to the year 2015 and every aspect of our lives is being bombarded with suggestive behavior patterns that promote consumerism beyond your wildest dreams. Drugs, alcohol, and tobacco are not blatantly promoted, but are done with a sophisticated subtlety that not even an adult mind is immune to. So can you imagine the affects that it can have on the tender mind of a child? The muse as a collective; dance, art, music, the word, etc. are a gateway that can be used to enhance ones life experience or influence it just as well. These outlets become tools used by those looking to control our thinking by way of drug-induced experiences. It is important that we recognize that when dealing with all aspects of our lives, that everything is everything. Drugs are related to the movies we watch, the movies we watch are related to the music that we listen to; the music that we listen to is related to the thoughts that we produce. It is a system that must be mastered in order to integrate ideas into the minds of unsuspecting victims. Meaning, concepts are simultaneously promoted through all channels of communication, music, movies, magazines, talk shows etc. Along the way, opinions can become "facts". Drug use helps this process because we become that much easier to manipulate. In a lot of cases, a child's first sexual experience can be linked to the use of drugs. We have a tendency to think of mind control as some form of torture or programming that forces people to do harmful or dangerous things to innocent people such as random killings. When in reality we are all faced with levels of mind control everyday. Whether it's the McDonald's commercial or infomercials that make us feel inadequate, we are all subjected to mind control on some level or the other. Our teenage years are our most experimental.

We explore more freely then when we are adults. Our thoughts and concepts about life have not been fully formulated yet, so the sphere of influence in our lives, which may also include drugs, plays a major role. Most of the bad decisions made by urban youth are related to drugs or alcohol. It is not uncommon for a teenager to wake up in jail the next day with no knowledge of how they got there. The teenage pregnancy and dropout rate are directly related to drugs, as well as teenage prostitution. So-called pimps prey on unsuspecting victims, using drugs as the main catalyst. They get these young girls strung out and dependent on drugs, then to satisfy their newfound addiction, they put them out on the streets to make money selling their bodies. In most cases, when you get the teen to detoxify, the prostitution stops as well. This just further illustrates the mind control affects of drugs.

Drugs and Creativity

Whether we want to admit it or not, there is a large population of artist, musicians, writers, dancers, and other creative people who strongly feel that creativity and drugs are synonymous, and it's hard to refute these claims when most of the artist in the music videos that they watch and most of the songs that they listen to have heavy drug influences. The mind is extremely complex, and when we attempt to tap into our creative energy using the mind, we tend to use external vices to accelerate the process. According to some, it takes you to a different place. It removes the boundaries that the mind sets up to operate in this third dimensional paradigm. This may sound spaced out, but when someone is on drugs we tend to call them just that, spaced out, right? This is not to condone the use of drugs but to get a better understanding of why so many people and so many artists in particular use them. We as parents and teachers can act like we don't see the elephant in the room but trust me it's there. Don't do drugs is the politically correct thing to say, but why? And why are so many of the same artists that we deem to be role models telling kids not to do drugs, but they themselves delve heavy into drugs? Because they live in two different worlds: the normal world that we all live in, and the creative world that allows them to become whomever they choose. So when they say don't do drugs, they are not misleading the children, they are really speaking in code. What they are really saying is, using drugs for the mere sake of using drugs is lame and dangerous. Using drugs to help spark your creative energy that may otherwise lay dormant inside of you…well, that's another story. How many parents, teachers and elders are ready to deal with this issue? Better yet, how many urban youth want to be rappers, dancers, producers, or artist? So the real question should be; how many parents, teachers and elders are not ready to deal with this issue?

Teens and Pharmaceutical Drugs

What is the difference between illegal drugs designed to alleviate pain, stress, or for recreational use, and pharmaceutical drugs designed to do the same thing? According to the many teenagers who take them, nothing. More and more of our youth are hooked on so-called legal drugs than ever before. They are easily accessible and are not looked upon with the same criticism. However, the affects can be just as dangerous. Have you read the side affects of some of these pharmaceutical drugs? At times it would seem safer to keep the original ailment that you have, rather than take these toxic drugs; which can result in death. How are these children introduced to such harmful drugs in the first place? Usually, there is a chain of events that lead to such destructive behavior. A general scenario could go something like this: A child's parents feed him or her unhealthy or sugary foods, which can make the child very hyper in the morning. The child gets to school and cannot sit still or becomes very agitated or even violent over a course of time. The teacher who is entrusted to teach and guide the child finds it very difficult to work with the child and labels him or her a troubled child. At the teacher's request, the child is then evaluated and in most cases, diagnosed with A.D.D. or some other hyperactive disease and placed in a special class for children with learning issues and given a prescription for one of the many pharmaceutical drugs used to treat this condition. The child then becomes addicted to such drugs and associates solving all of their problems with the drugs that have been shoved down their throats for so many years. They even pass these drugs to their friends in social settings creating more addiction. This is just one scenario of many. Some children just watch their parents pop pills all day and assume that this is normal human behavior.

Every ten minutes there is a commercial promoting a pharmaceutical solution to many of the problems that plague us. Our children watch television too. It would be silly for us parents to think that they are not being influenced heavily by these ads. There are illegal drugs on many corners in urban neighborhoods, but there are drug stores on just as many corners in the urban community as well. We as parents need to be at war with both of them! We must take a more holistic approach when diagnosing and treating our children as well as ourselves. We must deal with the problems of addiction from multiple levels. The wrong foods can cause addiction. Continuously being bombarded with advertisements regarding drugs of any kind can lead to addiction. Our actions as parents, teachers and elders can help justify addiction if we don't truly lead by example. At the end of the day, drug dealers of the legal and illegal kind are making major profits off of our pain and misery, and we as a society are left with the residue of a generation of addicts who do not discriminate in terms of the type of drugs used. As long as they can stay heavily sedated and insulated from dealing with social, domestic or financial issues, we will continue to have problems with today's teens who eventually turn into tomorrow's adults.

CHAPTER 25

THE CULTURE OF TELEVISION

T he average child watches 6 to 8 hours of television a day. That's a problem in itself, but more so than ever before, the quality of television is more important that the quantity. The envelope is constantly being pushed by reality shows, tween shows, and music videos alike. Young minds are being shaped and belief systems questioned with every sitcom that chooses to use its platform to challenge our old traditions about sex, religion, and politics. Ten years ago, you would never see anything close to what we see today in regards to the sexual behavior displayed. Or even the mockery made about religion or social issues. What was once taboo for even adults when it came to TV programs is now common amongst the youth. Same sex relationships, drug use, and near nudity flood daytime television. When it comes to what is inappropriate, if we as parents and teachers don't say no, its like we are saying yes. If we do not protest this madness with all of the strength in our bodies, then we are accessories to the crimes being committed against our youth! We as parents are no longer solely the first teachers of the children. We are in constant competition with the television. And while we are at work, we are losing the battle.

The World of Animation

Long gone are the days when animation was just for children. Many of the cartoons produced today are geared towards adults, but at the end of the day…they are still cartoons. So children are automatically drawn to them. Here is where it gets dangerous. The leeway afforded to cartoon makers intended for adults is far greater than regular cartoons made for children. They are allowed to make a mockery of anything and everything under the guise of animation. Most people are prone to say 'oh, its just a cartoon'', but is it really? We are still influenced by the subtle messages being conveyed. The affects are even greater when our children, who are drawn to these adult animations, are watching. You can get away with almost anything as long as you place it into a funny cartoon. Family Guy is a perfect example of moral abuse in regards to its message. South Park is another cartoon that pulls no punches when it comes to stretching the limits of right and wrong, even the cartoons that are made for children tend to stretch the imagination in terms of its content.

In hindsight, even the cartoons of old like Bugs Bunny, Tom and Jerry, etc. were filled with violence and subtle sexual innuendo. As parents, we didn't pay much attention to Bugs Bunny dressing up like a woman to fool Elmer Fudd, but children of a young age are easily impressionable, so the decision to explore the boundaries of their sexuality may have been made ten years prior, while watching cartoons. It may not have been their decision at all, if you understand how mind control and programming works. This is not limited to the realm of sexuality. The cartoons of this day and time are filled with spirituality, time travel, multiple dimensions, parallel universes, magic, etc. and while most of us adults don't believe in such things, our children are well verse in the occult. Just watch an episode of Air Bender or Dragon Ball Z to be brought up to speed on the level of sophistication of today's "harmless" cartoons. Whether you choose to teach your children of such things or have no problem with them exploring their sexuality is beside the point. That should be a decision made by you and only you as parents, not the Disney Channel. Not to mention the bright colors, tones, and flickering images that affects our brains on a molecular level. Cartoons are not harmless in any shape form or fashion. They affect the thinking of our children as well as play a key and crucial role in the overall development of the next generation. The adult cartoons further sustain the mindset initiated as a child.

The Culture of "Reality" TV

You may say, well what does all of this have to do with urban culture? And to that I say, everything. Due to the lack of education, which leads to high unemployment rates, we watch more television than any other group. Equally important is our low self esteem and lack of true identity as a people. This makes reality TV more like fantasy TV And when you are a lost people, those fantasies can range from wanting to be rich and famous, to fantasies of a sexual nature, to violent episodes unleashed on your enemies. Even the sadistic nature of watching others suffer for the mere amusement of your entertainment purposes is fair game. So the spectrum in which our emotions can be manipulated is huge, and the writers of these so-called reality shows take full advantage of each and every opportunity to exploit us. African-American women suffer the most. They have been reduced to money hungry, materialistic, conniving women who will use sex to get what they want. They will stab each other in the back, and most of them don't trust the men in their lives, or men are considered dogs. The sad thing about it is, most of these lost women act like this for free everyday in the urban community, but now that it is a lucrative venture to do so, they are all way the turned up (as the young ones would say). Again, this balls down to economics.

Every aspect of our life is profitable to someone else. If we are in pain, there are financial opportunities to be taken advantage of via pills and alcohol. If we are successful in business, someone is usually behind the scenes reaping the benefits. If we are athletic, we are usually being exploited via agents etc. Even If we sell drugs, corrupt police are extorting us in most cases. If we go to prison, these are now privately run corporations that capitalize. When we die, they are now stealing our organs! I digress. Shock value is at an all time high so every year the shows get worse and worse when it comes to the level of vulgarity, sex, violence, and nudity. The reality of the situation is that reality TV is more scripted than your average sitcom. Yet we still watch it as if we don't know what the ending will be. Those who watch WWE wrestling suffer from the same syndrome. This doesn't mean that real injuries cannot occur on a fake reality show because they can and do. For instance, even though they rehearse all of their moves, wrestlers do get hurt. Or in the case of reality TV, real fights do break out. They have blurred the lines between what is real and what is scripted reality so that you and I become immune to the difference. Under this formula, who is to say that most of the world events recently were not scripted reality in which real consequences were suffered? What about 911? What about Sandy Hook? Is it that impossible to believe that these events could have been staged with thousands of people dying as just collateral? Sometimes the truth is stranger than fiction.

Let's look at what's real and what is scripted reality from another perspective. Wrestlers are actors; they perform in a ring for your entertainment. Yet when they are out living their regular lives they still reap the benefits of being actors in a scripted world. They are famous in the real world for something that they did in a scripted reality. The same rules apply to actors who kill people, save the world, and have fast car chases in their movie roles. We know that they are just acting but we still revere them in the so-called real world. So why do we get all upset when rappers do the exact same thing? Why do we hold them to a higher standard? Is it because they swear by the code of "keepin it real" which would somehow suggest that the 50 people that they say that they killed on their album is true? What about the millions of dollars in drugs that they claim they have sold? The truth of the matter is most of them are actors as well. The only difference is they get to write their own script, and most of them write an incredible script filled with murder, drugs, women, and violence. Because let's face it, who wants to hear about a rapper with a boring life, nobody. You wouldn't go to the movies to watch an uneventful, boring storyline either. Fantasy is the new reality, yet fantasy can become reality. Go back and watch an episode of Star Trek and tell me that what was once a fantasy is not indeed our reality today.

There is a term used in Hollywood by new an upcoming artist. The term is "fake it until you make it." In other words, give off the perception that you are successful, and sooner or later, with the help of the "machine" (TV) you will be. Even more important to your success is your audience. If they believe you are who you say that you are, then you are, make sense? Rappers do it all the time. They put out these lavish videos with fancy cars, big mansions, and lots of women. In the beginning they own none of it. By the third or fourth video, they own all of it. Your participation in their fantasy accelerates their reality. However, you have to be careful. If you are portraying yourself as a gangster or thug in the fantasy world, it can easily bleed over into reality, and then real gangsters and thugs will want to test you. And the end of the story can be tragic. Tupac Shakur said it best, "I didn't have a record until I made a record." The television provides the greatest stage to perform on because the size of your audience is unlimited. Let's call it the fantasy accelerator. Almost everything that we see on television is staged, even portions of the news. Propaganda is used to manipulate, convince, and sway peoples' opinions so it also falls under the realm of using other peoples' thoughts to bring about a certain result. Sports in general are probably the only thing that is not staged, however it is star driven. So it benefits each sport, which are corporations when the biggest stars win because that creates the platform for them to market and promote their stars to the public. Basketball in particular is a star-driven league, so expect LeBron James to win more championships. And expect all of the corporations that are connected to him to relish in his success.

The true reality TV is on the Internet in the form of YouTube, Worldstar.com, and other public submitted video sites where real events are being recorded in real time, unscripted and unrehearsed. Some of these events range from amazing sports feats, to bazaar occurrences, to horrible accidents. Our thirst for action and excitement of the spontaneous nature keeps us on the edge of our seats and produces a high that can only be achieved in real time by real events. Anything else is a hack into our realities timeline for the sole purpose of changing, or manipulating our existence for the benefit of a chosen few. This may sound like a stretch for some, but when you reread this chapter and examine what drives urban America to act and do what they do, you will find some of these points very much on point. Where a people draw their inspiration and guidance from is critical. Urban America is used to having their leaders selected for them, they are used to being told who to vote for, they are used to being told what to eat, what to think, how to dress, etc. Somebody somewhere is writing a script at this exact moment for the sole purpose of keeping urban America in check so to speak. Reality TV is a form of mind control. Whenever your reality or what you perceive as your reality can be altered by exterior events that are scripted to some extent, then you are not in control of your own reality.

The television/internet allows us to venture into a world where anything and everything is possible through the use of imagination, special effects, mythological stories, etc. Our inability to unplug from the source of these altered realities has become an addiction of sorts. In other words, the world of imagination, orchestrated by media outlets has created a maze-like configuration that has us trapped and unable to find our way back to our own reality. This is systematically done. When the baseball season ends, basketball season begins. In the meantime football season is already in full swing. There are always world events that keep our attention, as well as blockbuster movies that are released every quarter. There are hurricanes, earthquakes, and natural disasters. There are boxing events, presidential elections, and mass shootings all vying for every second of our attention. We have given so much of our energy to external realities that the inner reality of self has been lost.

CHAPTER 26

FROM ANALOG TO DIGITAL

This chapter will be explained in the literal sense as well as a figurative one. For instance, I may refer to analog to not only break down the technical terms of the word, but to express an "old" way of thinking, and I may talk digital to represent a new way of thinking, as well as some of the technological advances achieved by switching from analog to digital. This will just be the tip of the iceberg in terms of analogies used to express certain points when it comes to the age in which we now live in. In general the world as we know it is moving forward. It is becoming more and more automated in every aspect. It is being coded in a language that not everyone will be able to speak. Urban communities are usually the last to receive the upgrade. This is due to poor education in the fields of science and mathematics, no technological access, and individuals unwilling to teach the new language to a people that they would much rather just take advantage of. We have become slaves to technology. We have become digital consumers with no true understanding of that which now rules us. The more technically advanced a civilization becomes, the dumber its people become, and the urban community is at the very top of that list. We no longer have to think for ourselves, our devices do the thinking for us. When was the last time you actually had to remember a phone number? Our food is prepared digitally (microwave), our televisions are digital, our computers are digital, our cars are now digital, even our cigarettes produce digital tobacco! We have become a nation of dumb people with smart phones. We have to begin to think "inside" the box to crack the code. It's one thing to sit around playing PlayStation games, and something totally different to open up the PlayStation console to understand its inner workings, literally and figuratively. That's the difference between an analog thinker and a digital thinker. The only technological devices we in Urban America have access to, are the ones that keep us dependent on the very devices that we consume. We are quick to upgrade the devices that we use, but rarely do we upgrade our understanding of how these devices work and eventually govern our lives. Now when we apply this concept to life itself, we begin to see a huge divide in the urban communities, and this digital divide is greater than just the technological aspect of things; there is a greater divide in the mindset and consciousness of the people as well.

This quantum leap in technology and the language in which it is coded has gradually moved our society from an analog one to a digital one. We have been intergraded subtly with things that we commonly use and enjoy everyday. Let's take music for instance. When the music cd was introduced, we immediately looked at all of the convenience and benefits that it would offer. I admit I too fell victim to the technological advances of being able to skip over songs that I didn't like, and go right to the music that I desired. In addition, at least on the surface, the music sounded crisper and clearer even though the pre set equalizer only offered three choices, pop, rock, or hall. Yet digital sound is not really sound. Let me repeat that. Digital sound is not really sound. It is what sound would sound like if it were really sound. It is an interpretation of sound using 1s and 0s to represent actual sound. However, the true nuance and essence of music is lost in the translation. Analog is more of a natural feel musically speaking. It fills in all of the empty spaces left out of digital compositions due to digitals precise calculations of sound, and when you add in the 10, 20, or 30 band equalizer that each individual can tune into their own frequency with, we get sound that penetrates the outer shell and seeps deep into the soul of each listener. So analog has a connection to your soul, let's keep this in mind as we move forward. The same can be said about the advantages of the DVD, cell phones, computers, etc. They made our lives appear easier, but at what cost? Is technology the new form of slavery? How long could you survive without your cell phone? Even the poorest of the poor in urban neighborhoods have cell phones and access to the Internet. Public assistance and food stamps are digitally distributed. Medical records are now kept on digital files and can be accessed anywhere there is a computer. We are all "online" for the next paradigm shift, yet some peoples' broadband is greater than others.

For those of us who were raised in an analog world, which would be those who are at least 40 years old or older, the transition to a digital world represents more than just a physical evolution; it also represents a quantum leap in our consciousness as well. The digital era literally changes the way that we process information, and if you are stuck in an analog way of thinking you will get left behind, quickly. On the other hand those who were born on the digital timeline have the ability to grow and process information at a far greater rate than any other generation in this current paradigm. They were born with super broadband speed. Two year olds have the mental capacity to run and operate computers, cell phones, and tablets, while older people from the previous paradigm are still struggling to adjust. This new generation is in what I like to call the "quickening". There ability to process, transmute, adapt to, and evaluate information is amazing. In other words, the digital era in which they were birthed is moving so fast that they don't even have time to develop long lasting negative thought patterns which at times can create stagnation. They keep it moving. While those of us birth during the analog era continue to suffer from things that have happened long before most of us were even born! This is based on our inability to mentally let things go. We feel too much pain and suffering. So that pain sits on our "hard drive" and can be accessed at any given time if the right codes are entered. However, it's not all of our fault. Remember, analog fills in all of the blank or empty spaces, so we have a complete understanding of our history in this country and abroad. We feel compassion for all of humanity. Digital information is precise, so while this generation may have all of the "facts" regarding our story, they lack the emotional connection that binds us together. They can't "feel" the music of life so to speak. They have become Dr. Spock-like in their interpretation of life. It has to all "add up" to make sense to them.

Those of the analog era are still holding on to the traumatic events of slavery, the Civil Rights movement, and other racial and biased events that have plagued Black people in this country. It is deeply imbedded within their DNA. They can feel it like it just happened yesterday. As a result they operate as if nothing has changed, which in some cases it has not. On the other hand, I know this may sound harsh, but those who were birthed in the digital era could really care less about what happened to their ancestors, or what happened yesterday for that matter, and it's nothing personal. They are just hardwired differently. New codes are being written every single day, which shapes their reality. Now they may not necessarily be the code writers, (I'll get to that in another chapter), but their DNA is automated to live in the here and now. So when they do not have an emotional response to situations that require one, we have to understand that they are functioning off of a different "operating" system. It has been said that this new generation is soulless and heartless, part of the reason for this behavior in my humble opinion is the synchronization of consciousness and technology has eliminated true feelings for life itself. This generation is not in tune with the universe. They function more like computers than humans. This is the greatest downfall of the digital divide. When we start taking on a digital consciousness, we become just processers of information, rather than interacting humanly with nature, the animal kingdom, and the universe as a whole. This generation's view on violence, sex, money, and life overall is an indicator of just how disconnected from a spiritual standpoint that they really are. We are on the cusp of a generation of human robots. Let's just say that analog represents the ancient world of science, medicine, philosophy, religion, etc. and digital represents the new age way of life, which has a different view of science, medicine, art, and philosophy. The more you study what is considered new age, you come to find out that is the ancient sciences being retaught to a new generation. So everything is one. What is new is old, and what is old is new. In order to understand what is new, we must study what is old. When we fully understand this science we will see that we are not generations apart; we are a generation rebirthed.

At the core of digital programming are the 1s and 0s. Well to this generation it is all about the 1s, meaning money and the 0's, meaning the lack thereof. This generation's ability to make money is like none other that I have seen before. In fact, they cannot comprehend how one can struggle in an era where so many opportunities to make money now exist. The analog or linear way of making money which is working 40 hours a week, waiting to get paid, and looking forward to two weeks vacation is unacceptable to them. They make their money quick, in abundance, and by any means. They spend it just as fast. They are not bonded to the money. They see it as just a tool to use at their disposal. So when you see them purchase what we would normally consider to be frivolous things, know and understand that to them, it's all about living in the moment. They would rather live lavishly for three years (digital) than to struggle for thirty (analog). Those who still view money from an analog perspective have fallen victim to the digital language of money, which is called credit. Credit is different than having digital access to your money. These are two different languages being spoken. Credit is digitally produced out of thin air, yet has to be paid back with real analog notes. It is an illusion, yet real energy is exerted to pay back these loans, and usually at a very high interest rate. As a result 85% of the population is left running on a treadmill, never reaching their destination, which is financial freedom. Urban communities around the country suffer the most from the digital warfare of money. Even the physical notes which are digitally printed are not worth the paper that they are printed on, yet we collectively agree to give this form of currency a mental "charge", which gives it life and energy. The urban community as a whole still suffers greatly from being digitally illiterate, however there is an emerging class of athletes, rappers, ballers, bankers, and geeks who are paving the way for a brighter future.

Now let's look at the male/female dynamic from a digital context. 1s represent the male penis or phallic symbol, and 0s representing the female vagina or sacred yoni. In its truest essence, 1s and 0s is the oldest language on the planet. It is the code by which we have all arrived here. It is a universal language used to bring about the "One," which is you $(1+0=1)$. When we tamper with the original code we may still be able to produce equations, yet they will not add up to the original code, which essentially assures the continued existence of life on this planet. The sequence of 1s and 1s, or 0s and 0s are foreign to the matrix of our existence. Yet hackers have somehow overwritten the original code and have gained access to a limited amount of numerical sequences that allow them to operate as 1s and 0s when they are actually not. These hackers have a lot of power.

For years they have operated in the shadows, recruiting many others along the way. Once initiated, you are taught to defy the natural order of the universe laid out by the grand architect, or the original programmer. The sequence of 1s and 0s guaranties immortality, but any other sequence is limited in its ability to live forever. However, the hackers are just that, hackers. They have found a way to survive by appearing to be 1s when interacting with 0s, or appearing to be 0s when interacting with 1s. Some of them are actually 1s and 0s at the same time! This has created an offspring of mixed numbers, and these mixed numbers have given birth to another generation of mixed numbers, and so on and so on and so on. As a result, what was once a perfect number system used to program this reality is operating imperfectly. At the root of every culture, not just the urban one is survival. The code and formula in which we have survived for years is being heavily challenged by a series of mixed numbers. Sometimes these mixed numbers lead to "improper" fractions, and the results are not always right and exact, some times there is a remainder. The remainder, or what is left over has to be factored into the equation of life on this planet at some point.

So the war on this planet for survival has begun, mixed numbers vs. whole numbers. The original programming states that you are either a 1 or a 0. You can't be both. The new programming suggest that you can be a 1 and a 0. Some would consider this an upgrade and some would consider this a software malfunction. The general consensus is in order to get a more definitive answer we must return to the source of the program itself, which states that you are either a cat or a dog; you can't be both. And if you are both, then you are a "cog" in the wheel of our continued evolution on this planet. We must seek to fight to preserve the original code that brought us into existence. We must not allow the hackers who are playing God to succeed in their mission to alter our reality. The hackers have at their disposal an external digital construct (music, media, movies) that has great influence on the minds of the people, yet we the people, whether rich or poor, from urban communities or abroad have imbedded within our DNA the original code. We can access it anytime that we want to return to the source. This is the one thing that places the urban community on even grounds with the most elite on the planet. Just remember that the hackers are always trying to crack this code so it is always open season on our young. However, this is where the older analog generation can save the universe. It is the universal language of love, which utilizes the 1s and 0s to preserve the code and keep it hidden from intruders. Without love we are just using the 1s and 0s (empty sex), and this make us vulnerable to hackers.

There is an old African saying that states, "Music is the gateway to the spirit world." I've often wondered if that includes digital music as well. Musical purists will claim that only playing live music, using real instruments can produce such magic, and since that's the way that it has been done for thousands of years, it is hard to refute this, or is it? The urban community may be the earliest and biggest vanguards of the digital era. We ushered it into the world on a grand scale. The advent of the drum machine in the early eighties served as an introduction into the digital world for most urban artist. We had no choice if we wanted to practice the sacred art of making music but to adapt to the ever-changing times, including the virtual world of instruments. We could not afford to purchase and learn how to play traditional instruments so we improvised, and the rest is history. While other groups may have used music technology for its convenience, the urban community used it out of necessity. Digital music was the first form of new technology that made its way into the hood. We didn't even know how to work the drum machines but the spirit within gave us the keys to crack the code of music from a digital standpoint. In fact, what we were able to accomplish using 1s and 0's far exceeded everybody's expectations, including the manufacturers of these drum machines, sequencers, and reverbs. We humanized the machine world.

Our ability to interface with these machines, in most cases without even using a manual, provided the world with a brand new sound called Hip Hop. After we mastered the turntables and created the crossfade mixer, which made two turntables sound like one, the next logical step in the Hip Hop evolution were drum machines and samplers. We could make a machine perform like a full orchestra, who else can do that? This is what you call alchemy, the transformation of something from one state to another. Now I will admit there was a time when the music felt and sounded mechanical, but now we have mastered the use of the machine world when it comes to making music. This brings us right back to the word love. Our love for music and the magic that it creates affords us the ability to make music out of any and everything, including with the body itself. This is what brought Hip Hop into a physical existence. Making music is making love, so when we were deprived of making music/love in the school system due to budget cuts we rebelled and took to the streets. This is why early Hip Hop was considered to be rebel music. The digital world provided us with a new outlet to express ourselves and it continues to help those who are considered less fortunate yet equally talented to have an outlet to create their own magic and share it with the world. As a result, the world has never been the same.

As I previously stated, every time we advance using technology there is a setback or sacrifice. In the case of music making, the synergy and spirit of the music has suffered significantly. Due to digital software like Pro Tools, no longer do the musicians have to be in the same room or even the same state any more to record. While this may be convenient for most artists who live in different states, the magic of creating something together is gone. Most may disregard the significance of this but being of one mind, body, and soul when creating is crucial. Do you think the Funk Brothers who created the world famous Motown sound could have achieved their signature sound if they were recording in separate states? The analog era forced unity. The analog era of music bonded many different spirits and souls into one, bringing about an entirely different energy manifested in the music itself. An even greater loss is our inability to hold an actual instrument in our hands and become one with it. The feel of the strings, cords, leather, and keys is essential in creating the magic that our ancestors spoke of. This is greatly manifested during live performances when the "tipping" point is reached where the musician and his or her instrument become one, opening a vortex that engulfs the audience and transforms the party or gathering into a ritual where the spirit world and the physical world become one. This is why even those who record their albums digitally are using live bands when they perform, because there is a difference. So when possible, it is imperative to initiate oneself into the science of learning how to play a physical instrument, even if you still choose to make music digitally. When we merge live instrumentation with the digital world, we are actually merging the two worlds, and maybe that is the key to us mastering both.

CHAPTER 27

MILLION DOLLAR LOSERS

T he economic landscape has changed dramatically in this country but not in the way that most people think. Urban-bred millionaires with no education, etiquette, and low economic IQs have emerged and bombarded their way unto so-called privileged territory usually reserved for rich white people and uppity Black people. Athletes, rappers, video vixens, and hustlers now show up at exclusive restaurants and clubs with rude, abrasive, and flat out obnoxious behavior. Not only that, they show up with an entourage of hood-rats with no social etiquette who have never been off the block a day in their entire lives. Let me be clear, when I say etiquette: I am not talking about acting like white people, I am talking about being able to govern oneself in any environment with respect for the rules and regulations of that establishment and its customers. It means to be able to adhere to the laws of the land. It means to be able to apply the universal law so that no matter where you are in the world, you can act accordingly. In other words, act civilized. Urbanites feel that money is the only thing keeping them from getting a place at the "table", and they are sadly mistaken. Yes, money is a part of it, but just a small part of it. It is used more as the initial deterrent or buffer to keep those that they feel are unworthy away.

In reality, it's never been about money, it is about exclusivity and elitism. It's about feeling that I am better and above you no matter how much money you have. Even some rich white people are not allowed in this inner circle. So one groups "come up" is another groups "fall off". When the elite have to sit next to a rapper at a restaurant that used to be too expensive for said rapper to patronize, they look at this as a sign of failure on their part. While the rapper looks at the same situation as a sign of success on theirs. The stench of urban America has now reached the noses of the elite and they are not happy about it. So now the elite have raised the bar. Now you have to be a multi millionaire of the highest level to even be considered, and this is just the deterrent! This eliminates most of urban America with the exception of a few athletes and Hip Hop moguls. The true ticket into their world is not money; it's secrecy. What takes place behind closed doors, and the exchange of information and knowledge that takes place is only for a chosen few. Most rappers and athletes can't hold water, let alone secrets of the highest order. Now those same restaurants and clubs that used to be deemed elite, are forced to cater to the clientele of rappers and hustlers in order to survive, even at the risk of having their establishment ransacked or even shot up.

The U.S. dollar is nothing more than a promissory note. Unlike in the early 1900s, it is no longer backed by gold or silver. It only has value because we agree that it does and our actions regarding it support the value amount. So when we deceive, steal, and even kill to get it, the value of it remains at an all-time high. However, our low economic IQs has us acting like dogs that chase cars; they wouldn't know what to do with it if they actually caught one. We have now reached the millionaire status in great numbers in this country and we don't know what to do with the newfound wealth. So we give it all back just as fast as we made it, diminishing the value of the very dollar that we worshipped when we didn't have it! Talk about being confused! This behavior only reiterates that we have a low economic IQ. By spending in this manner it feeds the economy, but starves our own communities of the opportunity to empower our selves as a collective. The economic ignorance perpetuated by these urban millionaires who only seem to see value in homes, cars, and strip clubs not only hurts them, but it also hinders our future generation of millionaires who only have the blueprint laid out by the ones who came before them. These are the ones that I call million dollar losers. Sure, they have the fortitude, tenacity, talent, and intellectual prowess to make a million dollars, but very few can sustain the economic success needed to last a lifetime. I've heard the Rapper/Actor Ice T say, "White people don't brag about how much money they make, they brag about how much money they give away". This is a profound statement on so many levels. Until these urban millionaires can brag about opening legitimate businesses in their neighborhoods that train, educate, and hire their own, their success will be looked upon as a failure. Not in the eyes of the urban community itself, we love when someone rises up from nothing to achieve great things, even if we don't benefit from their success personally.

The problem is this generation has been programmed to think solo. Their individual achievements are not connected to the whole. They are more prone to say "I got mines, so you get yours". Well, in a society that treats all of its citizens fair and provide equal economic opportunities for those who work hard for and deserve it, they would be absolutely correct. However, in this country we are a minority, so we must band together from an economic standpoint, which will then lead to the political power needed to gain respected in this country. Just study the Jewish, Chinese, and Italian people as prime examples. When we function with a "crabs" in the barrel mentality, this plays right into the hands of those who are staging economic war against us. One man's failure is another man's success. Our failure to enrich our own communities only succeeds in feeding the very enemy that we are fighting because it strips us of the very economic foundation that is needed to defend and empower ourselves in a capitalist society. Contrary to popular belief, votes don't get it done in this country, money does. Ironically, the economic status of black people in this country hasn't changed much since 1865. There has been an illusion of economic progress perpetrated by the media conglomerates, using high profile athletes and entertainers as the bait and switch. It is important to the elite that the most successful of our people are athletes and entertainers. It is also very important that these urban success stories are very high profile because it reinforces the dream state of the poor and less fortunate. It says to them that you too become rich and famous if you continue to make us laugh, dribble a ball real well, or buffoon yourself in movies. I am in no way suggesting that you should not master your art and be respected for your art, whatever it is. I am simply stating that it is no accident that entertainment is the only field in which we are able to prosper exponentially.

There is a thin line between being entertained and distracted. What is considered entertainment to the rich and famous that love to see us dance, sing, and perform is a distraction to most poor and under-privileged people who live their lives vicariously through athletes and entertainers. Sports and entertainment barely register a blip on the radar when it comes to true wealth. In fact, the last time a checked the Forbes List of the world's richest people, none of them is athletes, entertainers, or even owners of teams! Our greatest athletes and entertainers are not even putting a dent into the economic structure of this country and abroad. They are being used as tools to funnel future generations away from being doctors, lawyers, scientist, astrophysicist, engineers, entrepreneurs, etc. You would think that our only real options are to dance, sing, twerk, sell drugs, or shoot jump shots. So what good is it being a millionaire if it does not at least garner the respect, or place you in a position of economic power in this country? My Mother used to tell me about a running joke amongst white people about black people that went something along the lines of "What do you call a Black person that is highly educated, speaks well, and is financially well off? A nigger." Well if that's the case, what would they call a Black millionaire with no education, a low economic IQ, and a criminal record? I call them million dollar losers.

CHAPTER 28

THE PROTOCOLS FOR URBAN ECONOMICS

Whoat if we looked at boycotting from a different perspective? Instead of trying to bring down the entire system with one Black Friday boycott, what if we chose to do it systematically by boycotting one company at a time? For instance, what if we chose to boycott Pepsi and its related products, meanwhile, for those who drink soda, you can still patronized Coke and its related products? What if we decided to boycott Exxon gas stations but still purchased from Mobil gas stations? What kind of long-term affect do you think this would have on these companies and the economy as a whole? The problem with this generation, unlike our elders who came before us, they don't understand sacrifice. Our elders were prepared to boycott to the death. This generation is such slaves to consumption that they couldn't even conceive of the notion of not buying gas for a week. Part of this is due to the advertising sorcery performed by these major corporations. They have a unique way to make you feel that you cannot live without their product. A lot of their motives are targeted at your self- esteem. The other part of the equation is the media's constant attempts to keep everyone isolated and focused on their own individual needs as apposed to the needs of the whole. In other words, divide and conquer.

Divide and conquer is one of the oldest tactics used to keep different groups fighting each other instead of recognizing the underlining issues that we all share as the human family. Now the science of divide and conquer has been mastered to the point where individual against individual takes precedence. So when someone suggest that we boycott a particular company because of unfair treatment, discrimination, or sexual harassment, the first thing that will come out of their mouths is "I have to go to work", "I have to feed my family", etc. These are typical responses for those who lives in fear of not having, and in a struggling economy of this magnitude, could you truly blame someone for such a reaction? No. However, imaging being able to have your cake, and eating it too, imaging being able to sacrifice without sacrificing? Media outlets because they are short-lived events control the main reason that most modern day boycotts and protest are ineffective. As long as the media is covering it as a headline story, our interest and participation regarding said event remains high. Once the mass media decides to cover another headline story, (which is done systematically) we ultimately forget what we were fighting for and become susceptible to be programmed by the next big event. How many times have we witnessed or participated in a series of massive protest for valiant causes that receives major coverage for weeks, and then, out of nowhere, it all goes away in a matter of days, never to be discussed again? This is the power of the media. However, boycotting gas while buying gas is an unheard of method that can be used to reach our goal. We have the power. Not only do we have the spending power, but for the first time ever we also have the power of communication in our favor as well.

Through the use of social media, we can coordinate which companies that we will target and execute our plan until our goal is reached. In six months time we can have these companies eating out of our hands, literally. In the meantime we have to determine what it is that we truly want to accomplish by boycotting said companies. Is it to demand that more minorities are hired? Is it to bring down the entire company due to the toxic product that they manufacture? Is it to create a true political platform by showing our economic power to the world? Is it having these companies show their loyalty to our communities by building learning centers and scholarship programs? Or is it a variation of all of the above? The beautiful thing about this technique is that it will provide a surplus of revenue to the rival companies that we boycott while putting them on notice at the same time! Our demonstration of power and unity will send a clear message that their company could be next. In fact, we can stipulate to them that the surplus that is generated by us taking down their rival must be given to us to further our cause. So it becomes a win-win situation for the people. These methods can be applied internationally, nationally, and even locally. Do you know how frustrating it is to frequent an establishment that you know in your heart of hearts does not respect you, yet your dollars provide them with the economic power to live the life that you could only dream of? Those of us who live in urban America know all too well the feeling of being treated in such manner. We are needed yet hated at the same time. A slave plantation with no slaves is useless, a professional sports team with no players is useless, and a bunch of storefronts with no customers is useless. We have the power. So no longer shall we spend our hard earned dollars in any establishment without being treated with the utmost respect and dignity.

Which companies we choose to boycott first are irrelevant, as long as we are all in agreement. We can draw up a list of companies to sacrifice, while drawing up another list of the companies that we will support simultaneously. This system is foolproof as long as we do not allow the agents, uh, I mean athletes and artist who are being paid by these companies to sway us and knock us off of our square. In fact, we can apply the same concepts to artist and athletes as well. If we feel that a certain artist has disrespected our women, culture, and has portrayed us in a negative light in general, we can shut that artist down. Again, see the Jewish community for ways to protect your culture and image at all cost. And if the law is ever violated, the consequences for said action is dire. Imagine if we collectively agree not to utter the name of a particular artist in spoken, written, or in the cyber world for 90 days? Not only would that artist suffer, but the corporation that sponsors that artist as well.

These are the general protocols of urban economics but it is just a snapshot of its true potential. The first order of business before we launch such a massive campaign for true economic respect is make it mandatory that everyone reads, listens to audio books of, or watch YouTube clips of everything by author and economist Dr. Claude Anderson. He has been laying down the blueprint that we need to study for some time now. Our guerilla urban tactics must have a solid foundation and be based on methods that are effective for our economic survival. My dollars alone cannot get the job done. Your dollars alone cannot get the job done. But together we can shake up America one urban community at a time.

CHAPTER 29

URBAN VOODOO

What if the next time a police officer shot an unarmed teenager, instead of marching, protesting, and waiting for church officials and community leaders to organize and coordinate our anger, we did none of the above? What if the streets were empty, silent? What if we all stayed home and decided to print out a picture of the officer in question, then we placed his picture on a wall or alter and stared at it with the same intent? What if every urban community from the east coast, to the west coast, even internationally decided to join forces with the intent of shooting a violet flame from the middle of our foreheads, while all chanting "justice will be served" at the same time? That would most likely be the last recorded case of police brutality ever perpetrated against humanity. I know that this is a bold statement to make, but allow me to explain. The only thing that the rulers of the poor are afraid of is a unified field of thought that they cannot control. When vast amounts of people are on the same accord, with the same intention, and on the same vibration, miracles happen. Scientist have recently discovered and have been able to prove beyond a shadow of a doubt that meditation works. Entire villages have been healed and crime rates have dwindled due to the unified field of thought generated by the people of this same village who have practiced these methods.

Our current reality is the direct result of our unified field of thought being controlled by outside forces that steer it towards scarcity, fear, pain, struggle, and violence. Even major events such as the Super bowl are opportunities to harness a large unified field of thought for covert purposes, especially the halftime performance that is usually laced with rituals to heighten the energy. Ninety-five percent of the time when we march and protest, these are controlled events that have been mastered by our oppressors. The have put protocols in place to counter such actions for over 50 years now. The initial marches in the sixties were somewhat successful because there were no reference points or prior patterns that could be studied in order to manipulate the energy in favor of the very people that we were marching against. However, when was the last time that there was a successful march or protest that brought about real change? As previously stated, doing the same things and expecting different results is a form of insanity, so when we repeat the same patterns over and over again, our enemy doesn't see us as a threat. In fact, they see us as weak people who will undoubtedly repeat the mistakes of the past. We will scream "no justice, no peace" and then go home. What we fail to realize is that the universe is neutral, it doesn't take sides, and it only obliges those who know, respect, and apply the universal laws. It is also very literal, so we use our unified field of thought to scream "no justice, no peace", that's exactly what we get: no justice and no peace.

Anger is a form of energy that can be processed into a food source for those who feed on that type of negative energy. So when we march and protest we are actually empowering our enemy. Yet when we do not follow the norm and break from the expected patterns, we automatically change the outcome. When we go inward instead of expressing outward we tap into a different type of energy source. This is how we perform what I like to call urban voodoo.

The indigenous people of this planet did not just believe in magic, they knew, understood, and practiced the principles of magic. We are those indigenous people. We have forgotten more than most people will ever know about the spirit world and the energies that exist beyond the physical realm. With all of that being said, we still practice and perform the same exact rituals that our ancestors did everyday; we just have lost the intent and true purpose of why we are practicing our magic. Our ancient rituals consisted of music, dance, chanting, alcohol (spirits), hallucinogens (drugs), and sex… all with a unified field of thought. Urban communities around the world are performing these same rituals but with no specific intent and no unified field of thought, so the energy is wasted, or better yet used by those who have turned the ignorant into talisman for their own rituals that usually benefit their own agenda. Anyone can be turned into a talisman. Not the traditional one that you would stick pins into to harm or control, but the ones that you stick ideas into to harness and control.

How many times have opportunists come to the urban community with the sole purpose of finding a rapper, dancer, singer, or writer to make himself rich? Or to find a basketball player, who when placed in the proper environment will become a superstar? We are the most talented people on the planet, which means we are also the most magical people as well; so finding a suitable talisman that can be "charged" for a specific purpose is easy. Charging an urban talisman could be as simple as providing food, clothing, and shelter to ease the stress of everyday life, which allows one to focus on his or her talent. That talent can then be harvested, nurtured, promoted and packaged for mass consumption, making the one who planted the seed very rich in the process. However, this process can also work when applied in the exact opposite way as well. An extremely stressful environment can be manufacture to add pressure to the talisman, which will create one of two scenarios; pressure busts pipes, or pressure creates diamonds. If it's a rapper talisman being created, some studio time can be provided, along with his or her favorite drug and drink of choice, and some women. Then sit back and watch the magic take place. If it's a basketball player, some tutoring may be necessary, a better school with a nationally ranked team, along with the perfect home environment to stay focused and away from drugs and alcohol. This will keep the talisman focused on whatever they are programmed to do. It is important that the potential talisman has no idea that they are being used for a separate agenda, they must feel that all that they are accomplishing is of their own doing, meanwhile, the handler or programmer is in charge the whole time.

Billions of dollars are generated every year using this method of charging a talisman, and the pool of resources are unlimited as long as there are urban communities to be exploited. This is a form of urban voodoo that is perpetrated against us. Yet urban voodoo works both ways, (we'll get to that later). It is no secret that the greater the talisman, the greater the power, and the greater the results that can be achieved. For instance, certain rappers and athletes are superiorly gifted, and if programmed with a "super charge" they can reach superior heights. This "super charge" may require the normal ceremonial tools of magic performed at any other ritual like sex, drugs, and chants, but performed in an abnormal way. For instance, the sexual acts may be of a perverted nature so vile that they can never be mentioned outside of the ritual. This is done to access "portals" of energy that would normally be closed in order to thrust the talisman to new heights. They may also be given a series of powerful chants that summon up entities that assist the handler in achieving their goals. If the talisman agrees to participate, he or she will be initiated and rewarded with all of the fame, fortune, and earthly realm desires that they could ever imagine. They then become super-talisman. These super-talismans control all other talisman and potential talisman. The handler or programmers of these super-talismans yield great power. They know that they do not need to control millions, but have control over one that does control millions. Through their talisman they control what you eat, what you wear, what you buy, and most importantly, what you think. One wave of the talisman, and abracadabra, lives are changed.

All indigenous are potential talisman, and those who study urban voodoo is well aware of it. We are the ones who do not know thyself. There is a calculated effort globally to ensure that you never know who you are and the power that you truly possess. Magic has nothing to do with status, the rich, the poor, and the middle class all have access to the same stream of energy, if they are indigenous people. All others have to join secret societies or create talisman to gain access to the magical realms. There is only one secret and that is you shall never know that we, the people, no matter how poor, desolate, uneducated, and deprived are the ones who are really in control. As long as this secret is never revealed, they can continue to appear in control, and through their secret societies, they have a unified field of thought to keep it that way.

Now, I am in no way suggesting that the only way to be successful in this world is to participate in perverted rituals or that you must have a handler to open doors for you. In fact, there are more successful people in this world who have charged their own talisman with hard work, dedication, and commitment to their profession. I am speaking specifically to those who yearn to be rich and famous, which requires some dealing with Hollywood, the music industry, the fashion industry, a major sports franchise, etc. In these fields it doesn't necessarily matter how talented you are, at some point you will encounter an agent or handler along the way that serve as the gatekeepers to your destiny, I guarantee it. They know what you do not, which are the stereotypical depictions of us dancing, singing, and jumping is much deeper than just entertainment or cooning. They know and understand that with the proper knowledge of who we are, these same acts of dancing, singing, and rapping are magical rituals that can be performed for a greater cause. So they keep us focused on earthly matters and in pursuit of earthly treasures, which they themselves have dominion over.

The unified field of thought of most rappers is to make a hot record, sell millions of copies, get rich and famous, and have lots of women. As a collective, they are able to create this reality, yet they only receive a portion of the wealth that they accumulate because the handler and its constituents, the record labels, promoters, etc. receive the bulk of it, all while remaining anonymous in most cases. In corporate America, this situation is reversed. The handler (boss) takes all of the credit while the talisman is the one that most likely came up with the brilliant ideas that propelled the company to be successful in the first place. He or she remains anonymous and rarely duly compensated. These handlers and programmers cannot exist beyond the earthly realm without the assistance of a conduit. This is why they created the talisman in the first place. It is also the main reason that they are always around those who study and master the arts, because these are gateways to the astral realms and above. It is also the reason why urban communities all over America are kept in a state of constant stress and duress. We perform better under pressure; see Hip Hop as a prime example. And no matter how bad the economic situation is in the hood, we always have an abundance of drugs which is a tool of magic, alcohol which is a tool of magic, music which is a tool of magic, and sex which is a tool of magic, all at our disposal. So the same things that plague the urban community are the same things that can free the urban community. It is simply a matter of one's knowledge and understanding. So once the stage is set, the only thing the record companies, movie studios, fashion industry, and sports franchises have to do is wait until we perform the necessary urban rituals to bring forth the next phenomenon to feed the world. It can be an individual, it can be a dance, it can be a new music, etc. Some will rise and go on to do great things, and some will fall victim to the drugs, sex, alcohol, and crime. Even those who perish still provide an economic stimulus to the country by feeding the prison systems, hospitals, and morgues. So it's a win-win situation for those who are in the know. So the question is, which urban voodoo do you do?

If at any given time a charged talisman begins to lose its charge by "waking up", becoming conscious of what's really going on, or just decides to have a change of heart, there are protocols in place to deal with that as well. Again, the same tools that elevate are the same tools that dissipate. They can discredit you by orchestrating a sex scandal, portraying you as someone who is strung out on drugs, or an all out media assault on your character to make you look crazy and unfit. And if all else fails, remember those rituals that consisted of perverted sex acts that were too horrendous to mention? Well, they secretly tape all of these events. Fame comes with a hefty price. Fortune on the other hand can be obtained rather anonymously. There are more unknown millionaires and billionaires than you could possibly imagine, and they choose to live a quiet anonymous life. Yet from an urban perspective, there is no glory in that, there is no notoriety in that, there is not enough attention given to just being rich. In fact, I am willing to suggest that it is more important for us to be famous, than rich and wealthy. It is the easiest of the three to obtain. Becoming rich in this day and time can also happen very fast. Yet, because we lack the understanding of how true economics work, that too can be very fleeting because we have a tendency to celebrate our fame by spending all of our riches to maintain the illusion of being famous. Wealth is the hardest to achieve, yet everyone's definition of wealth is different. Some say wealth is a whole lot of money that can last generations to come, and others say true wealth has nothing to do with money at all since you cannot take it with you when you leave this plain of existence.

There is a new generation of thinkers who are stating that health is the new wealth. If this is the case, then that requires the mind, body, and soul to be in tune. It is no coincidence that the attacks on urban communities around the world are against our minds (media), bodies (food) and souls (music). In order to be in tune and apply such principles we have to have a unified field of thought that brings about this reality. However, a unified field of thought may not be enough because we can still be divided along those thought lines. For instance, Christians have a unified field of thought, Muslims have a unified field of thought, Jewish people have a unified field of thought, Hebrew Israelites have a unified field of thought, The

Moors have a unified field of thought, The Conscious community have a unified field of thought, etc. so divide and conquer can still be implemented because each group has a vested interest in their own cause. We have to elevate our collective consciousness to a universal field of thought that brings all of the factions of our community under one umbrella based on the universal principle of life. This will not be easy to do since we have been programmed to fight each other. It is our responsibility, the poor, the righteous, and the so-called underprivileged to bring about change.

So let's make music with a spiritual purpose, let's dance with a spiritual purpose, let's have sex with a spiritual purpose, let's do drugs with a spiritual purpose, and let's perform our urban voodoo with a spiritual purpose, because if we don't, we will be doing these same things for someone else's wicked purpose and agenda. Would you rather work for yourself or for someone else? The concept is exactly the same. The body is an amazing power source that can generate enormous amounts of energy. How that energy is produced depends on the methods used to bring it about. When we make music with a spiritual purpose we make music that can and will heal, enlighten, motivate, inspire, and change realities. Now for every move we make to help free ourselves there are moves being made to keep us in the current condition that we are in. There are those who want to keep the music toxic. Not just the words and the intent, but the very frequencies in which we hear and feel the music. So our goal will not be easy, but we have a few outlets like social media that can assist us in our universal field of thought.

We need to designate a day on social media where all of our creative independent artists release songs simultaneously that reflect our mindset. Then we, as a collective share the music with everyone we know. Using these same media outlets, we need to organize a dance off in every city at the same time where we come together to celebrate life. If you are sick, we want to help you dance the illness away, if you are lonely, we want to change your vibration to draw that special person to you. The young sisters who choose to "twerk" to make a living already use this method of dancing, they start off broke, then they perform the "rain dance", and money begins to fall from the sky. Depending on how powerful of a dancer one is will determine if there is a drizzle or a thunderstorm! Yet we are too busy seeing the negative aspect that we miss the spiritual significance of the power of the body to manifest some amazing things.

This is urban voodoo at its best. The negative aspect of this comes about when we are taught and trained to belittle and disrespect the sisters who are performing these sacred acts. However, the rappers and ball players are doing something that not even I could fathom or understand, they are holding these sisters who "twerk" in high regard! Even if they are doing it for reasons other than the spiritual ones that I am trying to express here is irrelevant. That's the way the spirit works. In ancient times, the prostitute was held in high regard because she didn't just feed the physical nature of man, she also nurtured his higher self as well. Do not assume that all of these women who dance for a living are just feeding the lower, animalistic nature of man, some of them know and understand the true power that they possess, and the power that they truly yield over the spiritual realms, simply by dancing.

What if I told you that having an orgasm or what we in the hood like to call "coming" is energy that could be harnessed to bring about positive changes in our lives if done right? What if I told you that if you could focus and create a mental picture of what it is that you desire, whether it's a car, home, new job, health, or freedom at the exact time of climax that you could bring these things into a physical existence quicker than without doing so? What if I told you that if you and your partner shared the same mental picture and could climax at the same exact time, that this process could manifest results even faster? These are the basic principles of sex magic and tantric sex that has been practiced by our ancient ancestors since the beginning of time. In fact, this is common knowledge amongst the people who still reside in these regions of the world that have not been heavily influence by the western world.

Our parents never taught us this because they themselves didn't know. They spend most of their time trying to steer us away from sex for a number of reasons, most of them being that we are too young, or not ready for the after affects of such life changing experiences. As a parent of four children myself, I understand the concerns, however sex is the greatest form of creation. It is the means in which we all arrive here on this planet. All of us! At minimum, parents wanted to make sure that there was love involved with the process, but this is urban voodoo that we are talking about. We are fortunate if there is any kind of connection beyond the physical before we engage in sex. The problem is that we are releasing tons of orgasmic energy into the universe with no purpose or direction. Yet the energy is not being wasted. Those who understand its power are using it against us. Those who understand its power are using it to enter into the astral realms and above to control our dreams and to keep us focused on partying and having useless sex. Those who understand its energy continue to flood our consciousness with an abundance of pornography to keep us in a constant state of sexual indulgence to ensure that we continue to generate this atomic-like force that keeps them in power because we do not know or believe that it exist. So if we want better conditions in the hood, let's have sex on it. If we want to stop police brutality from now on, let's have sex on it. If we want to improve the economy, let's have sex on it. If we want to shift the power back to the people, let's have sex on it. But let's do it together. We need to have a national sex day where we choose an agenda that we can all agree on, (or most of us at least), set a specific time, then get busy! No more free orgasmic energy being released. On a personal level, work with your partner to generate what it is that you guys want to achieve. This will require a lot of practice because it is hard not to look at and enjoy the physical specimen that you are engaging with. Fellas, if shortie gotta phattie, it's gonna be tough, lol. You can even practice these techniques of focused orgasms by yourself, but if you are a male do not ejaculate because that will lead to a waste of valuable life force, "injaculate" instead, and watch your talisman become charged with a force so powerful that no external energy will be able to stop.

For those who feel that I am advocating the use of drugs, I am not. I am simply addressing the elephant in the room, and the elephant in the room is there is a large portion of our society, whether white, black, rich, or poor who use drugs in some capacity. There are more movies, reality TV shows, and music videos that promote drug use on a constant basis than I ever could in this one book. The government themselves promote the use of pharmaceutical drugs every single day. The difference is I am giving you the launch codes to your spirituality, and these launch codes can be activated no matter what mental state you are in. You could be in a meditative state or drugs induced state and still reach realms beyond the physical body. The protocols of urban voodoo require me to break down the alchemical process of using whatever is at your disposal to help you transcend time and space. In the urban community, drugs are one of the elements that is readily available, and if properly used could help in the process. Now with that being said, there are numerous reasons why one would use drugs including stress, depression, pain, creativity, casual use, etc. But rarely is the true purpose of using drugs, at least from a spiritual standpoint, ever mentioned, which is to see beyond the physical spectrum which makes up about 20 to 25% of the entire spectrum of light. Our two physical eyes represent the illusion, seeing beyond the illusion is equivalent to pulling back the curtain and seeing the world for what it really is, and that is that we are all energy and we are all connected beyond the physical realms. Our ancestors would use certain drugs to see beyond the physical reality in an attempt to understand our connection to the all.

Everything that our ancestors did was for a specific purpose, including the use of drugs to assist in rituals if needed. These drugs usually consisted of some plant-based herbs like ayahuasca, marijuana, or mushrooms just to name a few. The earth holds many secrets, and by connecting with certain herbs helps produce DMT in the brain, which brings about altered states of reality. DMT, or dimethyltryptamine is secreted in the brain naturally, yet if you are caught with it in your possession, you will go to jail! That's how powerful it is. So technically the body is already capable of having a spiritual awakening without the use of drugs. This would commonly happen when we were in a more natural environment and operating on a supreme level of consciousness, but we are not in our natural habitat, we live in the hood, a concrete jungle where everything is artificial, even the food. As a result we have lost our ability to secret the magical elixir that could open the door to other dimensions at will. Fortunately for us, the shaman or medicine man came up with ways that we could still have such experiences. Doing drugs should be just that, an experience, and one that doesn't happen often. How many times have you heard a crack or heroin user say that the very first time that they used was blissful or magical? They say that it was indescribable. Unfortunately they spend the rest of their lives trying to get back to that blissful place, and in most cases they never do. Imagine if they were fully aware of the journey before they took it, and upon arriving at that blissful place, they were able to receive transmissions beyond this realm? That's an experience! Trying to have the same experience again and again is not really an experience anymore; you are now forming patterns trying to relive that experience.

Patterns form habits, and patterns are what make us slaves, even good patterns can be harmful. For instance, working out every day is a "good" pattern, but based on the initial results of your new body, you are now forced (slave) to work out every day to maintain what you have obtained or you will lose what you have gained. This is what has happened to the spiritual use of drugs today. The constant use and abuse of drugs have made the body immune to the process of being able to use them as a vessel for spiritual awakenings. The constant use and abuse of drugs has watered down the experience needed to reach new heights. This process is no different than receiving the flu vaccine. When you receive the flu vaccine, they give you the flu to make your body immune to the flu. We have abused the use of drugs and alcohol so much that we are now immune to the magic that these drugs once created. Now we are just drug dependent. If you drink alcohol everyday you are an alcoholic, if you use drugs everyday you are an addict. If you have sex everyday you are a fiend. You are not the high priest or urban shaman that can use these tools ritualistically to elevate yourself to new plateaus. Our urban voodoo has been deemed useless, so now the average drug user is just looking for a buzz to stimulate their physical needs. No longer are they looking for spiritual breakthroughs.

Our open enemy is fully aware of our inability to perform the necessary rituals of the ancients. By them flooding our urban communities with an abundance of drugs and alcohol, we are now forced to change the launch codes to take spiritual flight, or at least when it comes to using drugs and alcohol as one of the propellers. This new generation is hooked on synthetic drugs like "molly" which will provide a boost, but they are chemically-based drugs cooked up in some laboratory, which will have adverse affects on the body, especially those with a high concentration of melanin. Even today's marijuana is dipped in chemicals to create all of these new blends, which takes away from some of its potency. The difference is marijuana contains so many physical healing properties that it may be the one exception to the rule regarding everyday use. Just remember, when fire is added to any herb, it chemically changes the physical composition of it. However, the artificial environment in which we were birthed in has forced our bodies to adapt, even on a chemical level. We have endured far worse, including the crack era, which was designed to shut down our launch codes for good, and still we rise! Consciously and subconsciously we know that there is more to this world than meets the eye. So we are continuously trying to reach beyond the illusion of this third dimension. Our super-conscious mind continues to guide us and keep us aware of the true depth of our universal connection to multiple realities. Our adaptive mind continues to show us the spiritual potential of everything in our universe, including things that appear to be negative that can be used to positively lift us to new and amazing heights, including, but not limited to the use of drugs. I'm done.

CHAPTER 30

THE LBGT IN THE URBAN COMMUNITY

Here are my personal thoughts about the lesbian, bisexual, gay, and transgender lifestyle in the urban community...

What I feel personally about the LBGT community, and what you may feel personally about them is irrelevant! The truth of the matter is that there is a growing nation of people who live an alternative lifestyle either openly or in secret that are emerging from the shadows of our society. The urban community is no different as we too have seen a growing number of people who were raised on traditional cultural values choose to live an alternative lifestyle instead, for a multitude of reasons. I will attempt to address as many of them as possible, but first, let's deal with the elephant in the room: someone you know and are very close to is gay. Someone you work with is gay. Someone that you play ball with every Saturday is bisexual. Someone that you go to church with is lesbian. Someone that you respect dearly that you would never think is gay is gay. Someone's music that you have listened to for years is living an alternative lifestyle. Some of your spiritual leaders are gay. Some of your mentors, life coaches, and teachers age gay. Some of you favorite athletes are gay. Some of you favorite rappers, singers, and producers are bisexual. Someone you know that is always talking negative about gay people is gay. I am willing to bet my life on it! Now, this in no way suggests that you have to support that lifestyle, however, you do have an intimate relationship in some capacity with those who do. Your likes or dislikes about any group of people has no bearing on their existence. Look, if every group of people's dislike for another group of people could make them disappear, there would be no one left on earth! White people would get rid of Black people, Black people would get rid of gay people, gay people would get rid of straight people, Jewish people would get rid of Muslims, Muslims would get rid of Christians, etc., etc., etc.

There are those who spend an enormous amount of time and energy on breaking down the history and origins of homosexuality, whether it started in Greece, Rome, or Egypt. Then there are those who have done the scientific research that will show and prove due to the inability of homosexuals to reproduce, that they cannot exist in the future. Both of these studies are valid, but for the sake of this chapter, they are also irrelevant. Our people have a tendency to focus on two time periods that seem to keep us suspended in time itself, the past and the future. We are always talking about what we did in the past, "we were kings in the past", or "we were queens in the past". Or we are always talking about what we will become in the future, "things will get better in the future if we do this", "things will get better if we do that". Perhaps this is our way of avoiding our current situation, or insulating ourselves from having to address the current state that we are in. Torture victims use this method to escape the physical and psychological assault that they endure. Our elders, who were beaten, raped, and tortured here in North America, adopted these methods in order to survive. As a result of these out of body experiences, our perception of reality has never been the same. Even though to our ancestors, the past, present, and future existed simultaneously, we have found a way to escape our current reality timeline. We never deal with the way things are right now. We live in a state of present-denial. So it doesn't matter where you think the LBGT community came from or where you think they are going in the future. They are here now, so this has to be addressed here, and now.

Now the elephant in the room is about to get a little bigger. What do you tell a mother who finds out that her daughter is gay? Should we tell her that she shouldn't love and support the child that she birthed? Wouldn't that be counterintuitive to her natural instincts to love and protect her child? What do you tell a father who has been in his son's life trying to provide a strong male figure for him to emulate, yet he still turned out to be gay? Should the age-old principles of "a man should be a man" override his natural instinct to love his creation? What do you tell a pastor who's Christian Bible clearly states that homosexuality is an abomination in the eyes of God, yet half of his congregation is gay? The teachings of Jesus Christ has taught him to love all of God's children, are these not God's children? These are valid questions that need to be answered. For those who say that I am exploiting a sentimental loophole to get

The Black family to somehow accept a gay lifestyle, I am not. I am simply posing the question that everyone else seems to be avoiding. If we are trying to hold on to the very values that made the black family strong, yet behind the scenes, mothers and fathers who have gay children are sabotaging those efforts, or they themselves are secretly gay, then the foundation that we are attempting to hold on to or rebuild will only crumble. Disagreeing with your child's lifestyle and abandoning your child altogether are two different things. You may not agree with your child being a prostitute or strung out on drugs, but you will always find it in your heart to love them. Is this any different? Or should we round up every gay person in the community and oust them for being different? Should we continue make them feel unwanted, should we verbally and, in some cases, physically attack them? In doing so, we have contributed to what is now called the LBGT community. Or at minimum, we have forced our own to join forces with others outside of our community who have accepted them for who they are, or at least on the surface. We will get to the agenda aspect of this topic a little later. Mass movements are created when large amounts of people share a unified field of thought. In some cases, peoples need to belong is all that it takes. The LGBT community is a force to be reckoned with because they cannot be compartmentalized by race, sex, religion, or ethnicity. They encompass all of the above. Their movement is based on lifestyle and freedom of choice. One man's "trash" is another man's treasure. So what we throw away, someone else sees value in. traditional African families are getting weaker, and our offspring have joined forces with those of foreign traditions and are getting stronger. The elephant in the room is beginning to roar!

Let's clear something up: gay is not the new Black. When gay people have been beaten, tortured, murdered, castrated, hung, lynched, brainwashed, robbed of their culture, robbed of their language, and robbed of their religion, then and only then can we even remotely compare the two. As our illustrious scholar and child psychologist Dr. Umar Johnson so eloquently stated, "one group is fighting to be able practice a certain lifestyle, the other was fighting to be treated as a human being." This needed to be said because there is a movement that has taken place to give gays rights to marry, receive health insurance from their significant other, and a host of other rights that they are attempting to draw similarities to the civil rights movement. They are not the same. In fact, being gay and the gay agenda are two different things as well. There are a number of reasons why someone could turn out to be gay. According to Dr. Umar Johnson, who has counseled gays for many years, 95% of the cases he has addressed, some form of molestation had taken place. There are even studies that suggest that too much estrogen in our diets due to eating a lot of soy-based products has also contributed to the gay explosion. Then there are those who say being detached from your own culture and adopting the thinking and ways of a foreign culture can lead to non-cultural practices. Lastly, there is the passing fad aspect of being gay usually employed by teenagers who are experimenting with the taboos of life. All of these different approaches suggest that there may not be just one solution to addressing the issue. To be fair to gay people, from their perspective, they feel that there is no issue. This is who we are and this is who we will always be. However it is that they have arrived at their current destination, the truth of the matter is, they are gay. Most of them just want to live out their experience as they see fit. This is the life that they chose, and as long as they are not infringing on your ability to do the same, there should not be any problems. Then there are those who want to force their lifestyle on you and make you accept their way of life. This is where the agenda comes in.

Here is the undeniable truth that most heterosexuals will have a hard time accepting, if everyone who was gay or living gay lifestyles decided to all "come out" at once, your heterosexual world would be turned upside down! The sheer numbers alone would overwhelm you. With all of the political, social, and economic power that they have amassed over the years, they are truly in a position of power and are tired of being treated like second-class citizens. They go to work like heterosexuals, pay taxes like heterosexuals, start businesses like heterosexuals, and even take care of their children like heterosexuals. In their eyes, there is no "agenda." They want all of the rights that you have and feel that they rightfully deserve. Here is where things can get a little dicey. As a parent who is trying to raise their child in the traditional sense of man + woman = child, and then you send your children to school and they are exposed to children with two mommies or two daddies, how do you ensure that these children do not influence your child? Children have a natural curiosity and have a tendency to learn from other children. As a parent that is trying to teach their child good "Christian" values, how do you explain to them that even though the Bible states that this behavior is not favorable in the eyes of God, yet is accepted anyway? Television shows are now showing gay families in primetime. The president is an advocate of gay rights. There are openly gay congressmen. Rappers are wearing dresses and eyeliner. Athletes are now coming out and being applauded. The Christian church is accepting gay members. The Catholic Church is recognizing the relevance of the gay community. Pedophilia is now classified as a sexual orientation. The educational system is now teaching classes on the gay lifestyle. As for the parents who a trying to teach their children traditional values, it is becoming extremely hard to do so in an untraditional world. We are looking at an immoral world though a moral lens trying to make sense of it all.

Points to ponder, there is natural and there is normal. We, the original people of the planet, have always been in tune with nature. Our ancestors have studied nature to find our place in it. Everything we do is based on the natural order of things. Even living in a foreign land, in an artificial environment, stripped of all of our cultural essence; we still have found a way to realign ourselves with nature as much as possible. When we are out of order with nature, strange things can happen as a result of it. Part of the reason that we, the Black community have been the last to accept the LBGT community is because to us it is out of order with the natural order of things. We don't recognize it as something that we would naturally do. When something is natural it comes easy with no resistance, we don't even need to be taught how to do it. We naturally understand right from wrong. Anything that has to be done in the dark, in secret, and we are collectively ashamed of is usually something that is wrong in our eyes. When something has to be forced on a people, chances are it is not natural. It is foreign to those people. I can only speak for African people. Europeans may have a different point of view. What is unnatural for one race of people can be normal for another race of people. When things become normal they become accepted, however, that does not make them natural. Chicken nuggets are normal, but not natural. Surrogate babies are normal, but not natural. Microwaved food is normal, but not natural. Making music without actual instruments is normal, but not natural. In today's society, being gay is normal, but it is not natural. When you want to learn about the culture of a people, you have to study the so-called poor people first. They are the ones most likely to hold on to the traditions of the past. In fact, this is what makes them rich. In a lot of cases, the so-called rich are not of the culture, but have co-opted the land, and have stolen the riches and resources of the people. To ascend the economic and social ladder, the so-called poor will abandon their cultural ways and begin to mimic the culture ways of their invaders. Over the course of a few generations, there is a blending of the cultures so to speak. We begin to act other than ourselves.

There is a secret society in the urban community that very few people speak of. No it's not the "illuminati" or some "masonic" order that forces you to commit a gay act in order to enter. It's the rape of heterosexual men in the prison system. Many men are violated yet very few will speak of these violations, for obvious reasons. I am in no way suggesting that all men who have spent time behind prison walls have been violated because that would be highly inaccurate. I am not even suggesting that they would be considered gay if they were raped against their will. Let's be honest, if ten men held you down and brutally attacked you, there would be absolutely nothing that you could do about it. They are simply victims, but victims with a secret nonetheless that they can choose to seek help for when they return to society, or they can choose to become predators themselves and begin to violate other men. It is not uncommon for victims to turn into predators seeking "revenge" on those who violated them. Prison culture is a culture unto itself, and since most of the population in prison is Black men, the urban community is filled with men who know a secret. This is just from the victim's perspective, also coming home are the ones who were doing the raping. They too are being integrated back into the community. They don't consider themselves to be gay at all. They just did what they had to do when they were behind the wall. They prefer women, but will go up in a man if necessary. This is what we call the "homo thug" in the hood. They are very masculine, have lots of testosterone, dress very urban, and are even very muscular, yet will rather make love to a man or transvestite. This is a problem because their numbers go undetected, so we don't know how many "men" are operating under this code of secrecy. This is also a problem for the women who date these types of men, not only from a disease perspective, but also from a "seed" perspective. When a man ejaculates into a woman or another man he imprints his target destination. His ejaculation carries a code of his thoughts, spirit, soul, and essence. The receiver of the ejaculation is the one being programmed. It is also a feminine act to receive, even if a man is receiving it. When that man then decides to be masculine again and have sex with women, his own ejaculation and coding has already been altered or changed, this could lead to sexual confusion of an unborn child if one is conceived during the process. Then there are the one and done kind of men, who had a single gay experience, but returned to, being heterosexuals. That experience is still buried somewhere deep with their psyche, and somebody somewhere knows their secret. There is also an abundance of women who are turning the lesbian lifestyle. The stripper culture in our community promotes this heavy, but there are other factors that can be attributed to the rise in this behavior. A lot of this is also done in secret. When we factor in all of the men who are gay, on the down low, in prison, broke, homeless, murdered everyday, or just sexually confused, there is no wonder why so many women are turning to other women for support. Beautiful single women think that they have it hard fighting off all of the sexual advances of men everyday, but I think in this day and time good looking heterosexual men have it even harder since they are like endangered species. Women who are married to heterosexual men who honor and respect their wives and have the fortitude to fight off these aggressive advances from desperate women seeking to be with real men should be allowed a sexual release every six months or so with a beautiful woman of his choice as a reward for his honorable behavior. It probably would work wonders for the relationship. These married women are in possession of a rare gem or artifact. A true heterosexual man is a prized possession. Women who have men that "cheat" on them should take a look at the sheer numbers. They are heavily in the man's favor. He could be a man of low stature and still have thirty women beating down his door, so using unconventional methods, if he deserves it, to keep the relationship spicy could go a long way in preserving the relationship. Or worse case scenario: you could wind up with a man who is keeping a secret. The choice is yours.

There is a hood to Hollywood pipeline that runs through America, pun intended. One of the biggest elephants in the room that needs to be dealt with is; gays and homosexuals run the fashion, music, and movie industry. That's just a fact. These are the gatekeepers, or as I like to say, the "gay keepers". This is where they wield their greatest power. If you want entry into their kingdom you must pass certain test. Some of the more basic tests could include the "homophobia" test, which is the very first test given to those trying to climb the ladder of success in one of these mediums. If you display homophobia in any way, chances are you don't make it very far. If you pass the first test, you may be called on to advocate for gay and homosexual rights by denouncing those who are against it. This may include public service announcements, speaking engagements at public schools, or sporting events to promote tolerance for the LBGT community. One of the last phases may be to test your manhood itself. Yes the "casting couch" is real. The industry is famous for turning out straight men, and it's not as hard as you may think it is. When the carrot of success is dangled in front of ones face, (pause) you would be surprised at how many so called straight, heterosexual men fold like a cheap tent, especially when it is revealed to them that some of their favorite artist had to go through the same process. It becomes easy to rationalize this behavior when you get invited to an exclusive party in Hollywood for the first time and everybody there are the people you look up to and admire, and they are doing the unspeakable with men, women, or transvestites openly. Beyond the initial shock, you come to learn that the elite party differently, and you want in! The roadmap to success for most urbanites includes the fashion, music, and movie industries. You can also add the sports industry, who party with the same people that I previously mentioned. So at some point as you rise up the ranks of your chosen profession, the "gay keepers" will be waiting, and they are very particular about whom they let in to their secret society. There are millions of potentials from the urban community fighting for a few precious spots so the criteria for being accepted into their club can be vigorous to say the least. Those from the hood who are naïve to this process and do not conform are usually left on the outside. Now, do not become a "literalist", and take every single thing that I am saying about these industries literally. There are many artist, actors, and performers who did not have to sacrifice their manhood, or womanhood for that matter to make it in these fields. However, everybody knows that the LBGT communities control these industries for the most part.

Now let's talk about the gay mafia. Not a mafia in the traditional sense of extortion, gambling, murder, etc. yet a mafia that wields great power in the realms of politics, economics, and the music, fashion, and movie industries. They have the ability to get into your bank accounts, sealed police reports, phone records, and any other private portions of your life. They are here to protect their way of life at all cost. How many times have you witnessed an actor or athlete come out and make some disparaging comments about gay people, only to renounce those statements a short time later? This is the power of the gay mafia who can end your career if you work in one of the fields that they control. They move in silence. They are an anonymous force that will strike at your credibility, reputation, and lifestyle if you attempt to slander them in any way. By the time you realize who they are, it is already too late. Once you are on their radar, it is usually for life. There is only one other group who is more feared than they are, and that's the Jewish mafia. When it comes to the entertainment industry, I am starting to think that they are one and the same. There are two terms that you do not want to be labeled as, homophobic, and anti-Semitic. Your career in politics or entertainment cannot survive these labels. These words are used as weapons against anyone that these groups feel are challenging their way of life. Just because I don't think that men should be sleeping with other men, I am labeled as homophobic. Just because I think that some of the business practices of the Jewish community are biased towards non-Jews, I am labeled as anti-Semitic. While we are at it, let's add a third term to the mix. Just because I feel that White people have beaten, tortured, castrated, discriminated against, even murdered people of color in this country and around the world, I am labeled as a racist. Well, let me save each of these groups the effort of employing their normal tactics of slandering me by saying; I am homophobic, I am anti-Semitic, and I am a racist. Now that I have neutralized their first tactic, I am curious to see what their next course of action will be regarding this body of work.

Now back to the gay mafia. Their goal is not always to fend off "haters"; they also use their multiple mediums to promote their lifestyle. The entertainment industry is a tool used to promote agendas. Look at what is going on in Hip Hop today. You can't tell me that rappers wearing dresses, skirts, and halter-tops are not a part of some agenda to effeminize the most masculine part of urban culture, which is Hip Hop. Sure, women have always played an intricate part in adding balance to Hip Hop, but at its root, it is a male dominated, testosterone filled culture, until recently. When Hip Hop was an urban music form from the streets it promoted masculine concepts. I would even say that it promoted masculinity a little too much with the way it portrayed women as only objects of sexual affection. Once Hip Hop went Hollywood, it was a "Rap', get it? Young men growing up with no strong male figure in the home could at least idolize their favorite rapper as a sign of strength. The culture has been compromised and infiltrated by the gay mafia. Yeah, I said it! There is also a street element to the gay mafia that has emerged recently. Mobs of LBGT have been roaming the streets of cities like New York and Baltimore turning the tables on would be assaulters. After years of abuse, they are now fighting back. How long before the LBGT grows into a force on the streets that cannot be reckoned with? Imagine they began attacking heterosexuals for no reason at all. There may come a time when it is not safe for straight men and women to walk the streets. At the end of the day this could be a byproduct of the "hate" that hate produced. The elephant is roaring now.

We are all occupying the same time and space, yet we are all resonating on different frequencies and vibrations. New energies are being birthed on this planet everyday based on our thinking as a collective. This is that unified field of thought that I previously spoke about. New species are birthed as a result of our thinking as well. So we are responsible for all that we see because on some level or another, we created it. So before we begin to look for external excuses, we must first examine the internal source of our condition and the degenerative state that humanity is in in order to assess our situation thoroughly. Yet remember, what one group of people sees as a degenerative state, another group of people see as an advanced state. There are those within the gay and lesbian community who feel that they are the true spiritual ones. They feel that we are all androgynous beings but they are the first to reach those levels due to their ability to represent both male and female energies. They feel that they are the gifted ones; this is the reason that they dominate most of the creative fields of fashion, music, and movies. They feel that God is male and female, which mean that they are closer to God than any heterosexual could ever be. They feel that heterosexuals are old paradigm because they lack the ability to express their masculine and feminine energies simultaneously. It is true that we are both masculine and feminine. However, in this third dimensional paradigm we have been split into male or female during the birthing process. Since this is the realm of polarity, it would make sense that everything has an opposite, hot and cold, up and down, light and dark. By being out of balance, by being either male or female, we keep the universe balanced when we seek the opposite energy within each other. In the end, it could all be just a matter of perspective. Either we are advancing towards an androgynous state of a higher dimension where we don't need physical bodies any more, which is being ushered in by the LBGT community, or we are reaching the apex of a degenerative state of being where gender benders are threatening the very process in which life is created and sustained on this planet. Ok, maybe that's a little extreme, lol. Yet, in any event, major changes are taking place on this planet due to the physical, mental, and spiritual state of this generation.

CHAPTER 31

THE NEW URBAN AMERICA

The new urban America is not a demographic; it is a state of mind. It cannot be targeted as a specific location, it moves with the spirit of the people. The new urban America is not inner city youth struggling to make it out of the hood; it reaches all the way to Hollywood and beyond. The new urban America is not "street"; it's corporate. The new urban America is not just so-called minorities using sex, drugs, and culture as an escape, but White youth who purchase about seventy percent of all things related to urban culture. In a weird way they are paying reparations to our generation for the transgressions of their forefathers. The new urban America is more sub-urban than urban. Cable television and the internet has fostered in a whole new level of social engineering where even the most remote areas of down south folks speak, dress, and act like inner city youth. The new urban America lives in the virtual world more than they do the physical one. The world of social media is a parallel universe frequently visited by those who refuse to live a boring, mundane life reserved for linear thinkers. They suit up in their avatar, and launch themselves into the social stratosphere and become whomever they choose to be. Culture is manufactured in the new urban America. There is too much money to be made by studying the life of a people, then selling it right back to them in the form of entertainment, fashion, and movies. It is also a safe way for those outside of the culture to participate in or experience a piece of it without actually having to live it. The new urban America is admitted former drug dealers and current Crips sitting in the White House with the president of the United States. The latter even stating that he smoked weed while there. The boundaries that limited urban America previously are non-existent. Where our elders saw struggle, this generation sees opportunity. The new urban America is not about having a boss or striving to get a decent 9 to 5, who wants to do that? In the new urban America, anything that provides financial freedom is an accepted business venture.

Those who live by rules, morals, and structure are a part of an old paradigm. The new urban America breaks all of the rules, in business, creatively, and in love. How many of you could marry a stripper and be proud of it? They see the value in things that most of us do not. Strippers are beautiful, sexy, independent, and can raise your sexual energies to unreached heights, if she knows what she is doing. While most of us cringe at the very mention of Kim Kardashian and her immoral ways, she's flying around the world in private jets, drinking champagne, getting V.I.P. treatment where ever she goes, oh, and she's a multi millionaire. You can take your morals and shove it. When it comes to structure, if it fits, it doesn't fit. This generation is constantly thinking and acting outside of the norm. To them, structure leads to death. To the new urban America, conformity is slavery. The world of White supremacy is shaking in its boots as well because the new urban America includes their children who do not see race in the same manner as they did. They mix, mingle, party, drink, and have sex with urbanites on a regular basis. They even admire, respect, and honor Black super heroes from the basketball courts to the white House, and you want them to wage war against us? Good luck with that. White people are losing control. Part of the reason that we are seeing so many orchestrated police shootings around the country is that this is their last ditch attempt to keep racial tensions high to perhaps trigger a race war in this country. The new urban America doesn't believe in religion in the traditional sense, and would never give its hard earned money to some pastor so that he can go trick it on a brand new sixty four million dollar private jet. They party hard, drink, smoke, and have lots of sex, but they also study diligently. They would never accept the nonsense that our parents accepted about their existence in this country, in historical text, or on this planet. In the new urban America, everybody is a metaphysician, an occultist, a historian, a healer, an astrologist, and a hustler all wrapped up in one. You can learn more on the streets of urban America than in most universities.

The new urban America was birthed in the age of information, so general conversations about politics, health care, or economics is not uncommon, even amongst those who look uncommon. The new urban America doesn't believe in education, but is always in pursuit of true knowledge. The new urban America will not tolerate police brutality. They will not be caught dead marching down the streets singing "we shall overcome," they will fight back. The new urban America is prepared to die for what they believe in. They live every minute of life like it might be there last. That is what you call true freedom, how are you living? The new urban America will suffer a tremendous amount of collateral damage before it's all said and done. Most of them have incarnated at this time to party, smoke weed, and die a horrible death, that's their mission, what's yours? Sacrifices have to be made in order to ensure that the original people of this planet survive the next paradigm shift. This concept that everyone is going to make it is nonsense. The so-called bottom feeders, who seem not to have any regard for life, authority, and live recklessly, are just as significant as everyone else on the planet. Do not interfere by trying to teach, educate, or place them on a spiritual path, you are only slowing down the process. Allow them to fulfill their destiny so that you can fulfill yours.

The new urban America is the heart beat of the planet itself. Everything permeates from it, music, fashion, dance, art, language, philosophy, you name it; we create it. No one race, religion, or spiritual system can claim the new urban America. The new urban America is made up of the Moorish Science Temple, the Nation of Islam, The nation of Gods and Earths, The Hebrew Israelites, The Pan Africanist, The RBG movement, The Nuwaupians, poppers, lockers, rockers, and Hip Hoppas! The day will come when they realize that what makes them different is what makes them the same. The new urban America is the blending of multiple cultures into a new culture that the world had never seen before. For those who are stuck in a bubble and believe that they can hold on to their old traditional ways of doing things and viewing the world, you are in for a rude awakening. The next ten years will be like none other that this planet has ever witnessed before, so get ready. I am just the messenger.

CHAPTER 32

MESSAGE TO PARENTS

This may be the toughest time to raise a child. Never before have the odds have been so stack against our youth than they are today. Crime, drugs, and a failing educational system are just a few of the challenges that they are facing. The traditional methods of instilling cultural values in the life of a child have become extreme difficult due to the fast paced world around us. This includes information, technology, and spirituality. As parents, we claim we want our children to be independent, intelligent, free thinkers. This is a blatant lie. We want our children to think the way that we do, we want them to act the way that we do, we want them to live and work the way that we do, we want our children to see the world the way that we do. From an early age we imprint our children with our programming about life. This is what our parents did to us, and their parents did to them, and since we made it this far, we equate that with being successful when it comes to raising a child. In fact, all we have done is facilitate a series of patterns that we have instructed our children to follow, a blueprint if you will of ideas and concepts that will ultimately lead them right back to where they started, or better yet, where we started. This is the polar opposite of freedom. We are hindering our children and don't even realize it. We make fun of how white people give their children so much freedom, yet it has allowed them to see the world from a much broader perspective with unlimited possibilities on what they can achieve. They are free thinkers. However, I would be remiss if I didn't mention the traumatic physical and psychological abuse that our ancestors have suffered at the hands of white supremacy, which has ultimately played a major part in the way that they raised their children. We are the children of those children. Now we are raising our own children. We have been inserted into an urban matrix, which in essence is a course of continued physical, mental, and spiritual patterns that govern our lives. The longer and deeper the pattern, the more difficult it is to escape this urban matrix. Imagine four hundred years of thought patterns, eating patterns, love patterns, and survival patterns passed down from generation to generation. These are the ramifications of what we see today.

We have a tendency to blame our youth for the way that they act today, yet we, as parents are the ones truly responsible for their actions. The truth of the matter is we have failed them. We sat around while the police murdered our sons and we did nothing to stop it. We sat around and allowed them to miseducate and indoctrinate our children with European concepts and we did nothing to stop it. We sat around and allowed them to vaccinate and medicate our children and we did nothing to stop it. We sat around and allowed them to feed our children poisonous foods, sugary beverages, and cancerous products and we did nothing to stop it. We sat around and allowed the television to program our children with violent content, sexual confusion, and negative images of the Black family and we did nothing to stop it. Whether we want to admit it or not, our children see us as a bunch of cowards. We didn't fight for them. Then we have the nerve to tell them about the fifties and sixties when their elders fought and died for what they believed in. We tell them about Dr. King and his courageous non-violent stand against white people, even in the face of all of the violence that he suffered. We tell them about Malcolm X and the Nation Of Islam, which was greatest organization of self-sufficient men and women that our community had ever seen. We tell them about how the Black Panther Party not only started breakfast and lunch programs for inner city children, but also how they would arm themselves and protect their communities at all cost, even against corrupt police officers. Then when they take a snap shot of our current situation, they cannot help but wonder, what happened to us, their parents? Why won't we fight for them? At least their elders died an honorable death. At the current rate that things are going, we will just die.

Parents, we are at war. We are at war to save our children at all cost. We are the last line of defense against a system that is out to destroy our future by eliminating our children. Here are some guerilla tactics that we can employ in order to begin to combat our enemy's advances. One of the greatest gifts that we can pay our children is time. I know that this sound simple, but it is crucial. Make time for every game that they play in, every recital that they perform in, and every chorus that they sing in. If attention is the new currency, then attention from a parent or loved one is pure gold. While your child is sitting around playing PlayStation, play with them, even if you do not know what you are doing. The game is irrelevant. Time will give you the opportunity to listen to what interest your child, and when we listen, we learn. We get to learn who their friends are, what kind of girls or boys that they like. In time you will get to know what your child feels about drugs, sex, violence, friendship, life. Time has worked wonders for me. You have no idea how many games, ceremonies, and school events that I have sat through where they are celebrating mediocrity by giving everyone an award or trophy, and as a proud dad I stand and applaud is if my child just won an Oscar. It was never about the award, it was always about the love and support, which requires, time. This may be challenging for single parents but not impossible. Just cut back on some of the TV. shows and other nonsense that usually occupies ones time and you will be amazed at how much time there is to show love. When this is done early in a child's life, it literally changes the course of their life. All children want to be loved, and no amount of money can equate to time itself.

The conversation about sex must be moved up from the tender age of 13 to about the age on 10. This is a must because of the world of social media, innuendo of television, and friends and peers who are already in the know. This makes most parents cringe, but the sooner your child is aware of their sexual energy, the better they are prepared for how to handle it. The better they will be prepared to recognize a predator, the better they will be able to recognize subtle advances. The conversation has to be an extensive one (there goes that elephant in the room again). Love is the greatest energy on the planet and it is most manifested during the act of sex, yet parents refuse to have the talk, leaving their children vulnerable to hurt, confusion, and emotional pain. We think that time will solve the problem. Meaning, when they (our children) get old enough, they will figure it out. A child's first sexual experience should be something that they are prepared for physical, mentally, and spiritually. It will undoubtedly change them forever. Now I am in no way advocating that your child should be having sex at an early age. In fact, you should use those nasty pictures of beat up penises and mutilated vaginas on the Internet as a scare tactic if necessary. Show them the pictures and explain to them that this is what sex looks like void of love and responsibility. Then balance it out by showing them the power that they possess when they have sex that is filled with love and why it is important to wait for the right time and partner to express such love. This message is extremely powerful when the father, who is demonstrating these very actions by the way that he treats the mother, conveys it. For the parents who understand the power of sex magic, that is a plus because it ultimately teaches your child the power of creating and manifesting beyond the physical. It's where their super powers lie.

Truly understanding social media is critical for parents. Our children have the ability to create alter egos using social media that are cloaked in layers of smokescreens that make it difficult to decipher who they really are. Let's make something crystal clear: We are all under government surveillance. Just accept it. Now we have to put our children under mommy and daddy surveillance. We need to follow our children into the vortex of social media using fake names and made up identities if necessary. What they won't tell you they will tell their friends. In fact, you may learn more about your child by being a "friend" than being a parent. We have to become adept in keeping up with the ever-changing flow of apps and gadgets that they use. As soon as they find out their parents or older people in general are using something that they too are using, it's on to the next. If your child finds out that they are being monitored, they will be quick to scream that this is an invasion of privacy, but if I am paying the phone bill, I should have the right to know what's going on. If they are old enough to pay their own bill, then chances are they have reached an age where they should already have a sense of right and wrong.

That's one aspect of social media. The other side is one that we can all benefit from. Our children are already engrossed in the world of technology. The problem is it is for all of the wrong reasons, which is to be entertained, waste valuable time, and it is used as a distraction of major proportion. The difference between our children and techy white children is they see technology from a whole other mind's eye. They want to learn how technology works. This immediately puts them in a position of power because technology rules the world. So we want to play games and they want to know how games are made. For this reason, the financial gap between urban youth and techie white children is growing extremely fast, yet the playing field to learn how to program games has never been more evenly keeled. Parents have to adapt to this fast paced world. We have to find reasons to embrace technology because it is the future. There are free apps that teach people how to write code for video games and game apps available to anyone and everyone who wants to learn. I am getting ready to hire my nephew and pay him $10 an hour for a minimum of three hours a day to learn code. On the surface I am just putting a few dollars in his pocket, but because he wants to specialize in computers, I am actually preparing him for a bright future in those fields. At the rate that we understand technology, we are about to become cyber slaves. The traditional method of going to college for four years and getting an outdated degree is over. All things are possible with the technical know how. Understanding technology requires a certain understanding of mathematics. Understanding mathematics leads to a greater understanding of how the universe works. Understanding how the universe works leads to a greater understanding of spirituality. Everything is everything.

Now let's talk spirituality. Not religion, but your spiritual birthright. Real spirituality cannot be taught to you, it is innate. It is encoded within you very essence. We are spiritual beings having a human experience. We are so much more than the physical flesh. Your body is just a suit, or an avatar if you will, that you use to interface with other humans here on earth. You are pure energy that could never be destroyed. You exist everywhere and you exist nowhere. So when a child incarnates on this planet, the first question that should be asked is "why are you here?" Our ancestors would ask this very question to the unborn child being carried in the mother's womb. Through spiritual channels the child would convey whether they were the reincarnation of a king, or a warrior, or a great musician, etc. when the child is physically born, the village would prepare the child for his or her destiny be making the things that they need to harness their skills readily available. Parents, your unborn child chose you, not the other way around. So there is a responsibility to love, protect, and assist the child on their earthly mission. You are their guardian in ways that most couldn't even imagine. From an early age, pay very close attention to what interests your child. Then do everything in your power to ensure that nothing interferes with their training. By the age of six or seven, if you are paying attention, you should have some idea of what your child is here on earth to do. After that, the child is fully inserted into the matrix, which makes it difficult to accomplish the goal of steering them to their destiny. Once the exterior forces go to work, the climate in which is needed to harness the skills and purpose of a child becomes almost impossible. This is about climate control. All of the chaos and confusion, or what appears to be confusion is skillfully orchestrated to ensure that our future incarnates who have been summoned to this planet to assist us in our universal pursuit of freedom, justice, and equality never know who they are, or what their mission is.

Most parents have no idea what I am talking about, and here in lies the problem. If we only teach our children that they are human and their mission in life is to go to school, get a job, have children, and live some mundane life, then that is all that they will aspire to do and be. If we teach them from the beginning that their life has purpose and they are here to change the world, they will aspire to do just that. We have to teach them that just to get to earth was an amazing feat. By beating out billions of other potential sperm cells is an accomplishment worth being proud of and never taking for granted. When this is realized, they begin to realize that they are the "one". In the early stages of life, they know why they are here, but we sabotage their lives with all of the fear and confusion that stopped us from achieving our own mission. We dumb them down until they simply forget why they are here. We have failed them physically, mentally, and spiritually. Ignorance of the spiritual law is no excuse. It is our spiritual responsibility to raise conscious children who are aware of their purpose here. If not, the results are what you see going on in these streets everyday. Sending your children to church can kill their spirituality. Sending your children to school can kill their spirituality. Feeding our children the wrong foods can kill their spirituality. Listening to the wrong kinds of music can kill their spirituality. This message is for parents, who truly care about their children and their future, and are willing to fight for them at all cost, not for parents who could care less about their children by allowing them to raise themselves, feed themselves, and care for themselves. For those types of parents who party more than parent, whose priorities are ass backwards, and who would rather sit around and do nothing to help their children, there is absolutely no hope for you or your children. In fact, good luck to you.

CHAPTER 33

MESSAGE TO TEACHERS

The very first thing that each teacher should wonder about every child that enters her classroom is, why are you here? This may seem like a rhetorical question, but it is not. Each child is in a teacher's class for a multitude of reasons that are not immediately known by the teacher. I came to school to ensure that I would get at least two meals a day, which was breakfast and lunch because dinner in my household was not guaranteed. That was my primary reason. I also came to school to escape the harsh reality of being a neglected child, whose father was not around, and whose mother was an intravenous drug user. So I could care less about books that read, "see Jane run" when my father was actually on the run. School provided me with at least eight hours of solace, and in the process I might learn something. There were a few teachers who over the course of time came to understand my situation and provided comfort that went way beyond learning my ABCs. These were the teachers that I worked really hard for in spite of my domestic situation. They showed that they actually cared for me and I didn't want to let them down. I did well in school so that my mother wouldn't have to come there, how crazy is that? I knew if I excelled there would be no reason for her to show up and embarrass me by leaning and nodding all over the place, looking like a drug addict in front of all of my friends. If I did well she would only have to show up for special ceremonial occasions when there would be so many people around that maybe no one would notice her. The reason that I am telling you teachers this story is because I represent every single inner city youth who is facing similar problems, yet have to put on a brave face and come to school and act like everything is great. I represent every child who has a crack head mother at home, or an abusive father, or an uncle who is molesting them. I represent every child who has domestic issues that make learning academically challenging. Our children are constantly in survival mode. Very few are able to come to school with a clear mind, focused and ready to learn the lessons of the day.

After the child navigates his way to school and finally settles down, he can't help but look to the front of the classroom and wonder, as he stares at the teacher and says "why are you here? The typical teacher from the urban community is female and Jewish. Not only does she not live in the community, her own children would never be caught dead going to one of these schools. These Jewish women are so far removed from the urban experience that it is a disservice to have them even attempt to teach our children anything. In order to teach the child, you must first be able to understand, and then reach the child. Yes, most of our urban schools have teachers who look like their students as well, but the numbers are pale in comparison to that of the Jewish persuasion. These are just the facts. The cultural divide between the Jewish community and the so-called Black community leads me to wonder, what's the real premise of this relationship? Do Jewish women really love inner city children so much that they would forfeit an opportunity to work in their own communities, teaching their own, making much more money? Let me not just target one ethnic group, White, Anglo Saxon teachers are in the same category. Do you love inner city youth so much that you make the ultimate sacrifice of trekking all the way from the suburbs to teach them because you truly want to see them do well in life? If not, then why are you here? If so, then why are our children failing at an alarming rate in the schools in which you are the majority? Most will be quick to state that the children are violent, inattentive, unfocused, and have no respect for authority. Therefor teaching them is almost impossible, yet they still apply for these positions in great numbers. If I didn't know any better I would say that it's not about teaching our babies, more than it's about monitoring, miseducating, and culturally confusing them. I'll ask the question again, white teacher, Jewish teacher, why are you here? This is not a racist rant. You would never allow minorities to flock to your suburban towns and teach your children. Never. How would it feel to walk through the halls of your child's school and see nothing but Black men at the head of the class teaching your babies about their history, and preparing your children for the future? I didn't think so. In order to teach our children, you first have to love our children, understand our children, relate to our children, want the absolute best for our children, and most importantly, look like our children.This is the prerequisite to even be considered for the position of teacher of urban children. So I will ask the question for the last time: Why are you here?

Now, for those who have meet the criteria to teach our children, we have a different set of issues that must be addressed. Let's get the obvious out of the way first, where are all of the positive male teachers? Our young men suffer the most because there are no men in their first home and there are not enough men in their second home, which is school. This is critical because we lose our young boys early. Their disinterest and behavior problems can be attributed to not seeing and interacting with enough positive men on a regular basis. By eliminating the teachers that do not love our children and do not look like our children only addresses half of the problem. We need balance in our school systems. The subject in whom a male teacher teaches is one thing, his presence serves an entirely different purpose all together. Most male teachers are relegated to the gym or coaching a team, and this is unacceptable. They have to become more involved. When I see strong male figures around young men, the young men are usually disciplined, focused, and have a sense of direction. That's if the male accepts the responsibility that he is the father of a community rather just his own children. Our women teachers are doing the best that they can by providing the academic lessons needed to further their education, as well as the motherly support, but they cannot teach our boys to be men. More men need to apply for these positions because it is spiritually rewarding to do so. In some cases, a male teacher may be the first interaction a young fatherless child has with a man, period. It really does take a village to raise a child.

There are a few other factors that I feel are important for teachers to consider when they are dealing with children of the inner city. Most of their diets are extremely poor. Their morning usually starts with a bowl of sugary cereal, and then they hit the corner store of bodega and buy a bunch of sugary snacks. By the time they get to school they are fully charged with sugar. Not only is this bad for their health in general, it also make their attention spans very short. They become fidgety, hyper, and disruptive. Over the course of time, a teacher's patience may run thin and she may recommend to the parents or upper faculty that the child in question may need to be evaluated for ADHD. As Dr. Umar Johnson states, this is a huge mistake. We are burying our young men before they even have a chance. Once they are medicated and sedated, their life is basically over. They are labeled as troubled children, passed from one special education class to the other until the child decides to give up on school altogether. In the past, we would never give up on our children. We would never call on the state for help, we as a community dealt with it. Parents are also complicit because they are looking to get a check for the child from the government. So again, when it's all said and done, we are failing our youth.

Teachers have to be mothers, fathers, social workers, psychologist, cooks, spiritualist, volunteers, and a litany of other things in order to successfully raise our children. I applaud those who have accepted the responsibility even though the financial compensation for doing so in never realized. You are our communities true shining lights. Our children are not dumb. They know which teachers love them and which ones are there just to get a paycheck, and that includes the one who look like them as well. They also know that most of the curriculum being taught to them is not conducive for them, and that's putting it nicely. So teachers have to come off of the beaten path to fully engage them. This may be hard since most of our teachers have been conditioned to train our children to pass tests, or recondition them to follow the rules of a common core curriculum. However, that is not how our children learn. Urban teachers need to condense their lessons to math, science, language, and our history. Then they need to add a couple of life classes like, domestic violence, drug use and abuse, sex prevention, and an urban tactical class, like how to avoid getting shot by the police. Then they need to add an arts class. Here is where they get to practice and understand the true significance of the arts. If the art class is taught correctly, this will lead to the child understanding their spiritual significance in this world. The rest of those courses get be thrown in the garbage. Teachers have to recognize the individualism of each child and have different demands and expectations for them. A child with extremely poor living conditions and no home support, but can memorize his homework should be given just as much credit for completing the lesson as a child who studied, researched, and typed the assignment. If a child can sing the homework, let them sing it, if a child can draw the homework let them draw it, if a child can rap his homework and it is filled with all of the facts and details, then they should be given some kind of credit for their effort. Teachers have to meet the children where they are mentally, then raise the bar of expectation and have the child ascend to where they need to be.

The physical make up of the urban school system needs an extreme makeover as well. Most of the schools resemble prisons. The lighting, the dull paint on the walls, the big beefy security guards, and the metal detectors all point to a prison mentality. When a student enters the building and is forced to stand in a single line, empty out their bags, go through the metal detector, and be physical scrutinized, this subconsciously prepares him or her for what prison life is like. When this is coupled with the actual violence, drug selling, gang activity, and sexual assaults that take place on young women, it paints a clear picture of what the future holds for most of them. Teachers and staff have to make the schools more inviting. They have to make it a place that students look forward to coming to. When you change the vibration, you change the vibration. Parents who visit their children's school should not be subjected to the same treatment as their children are because it looks like they are visiting their child in prison rather than in school. The school to prison pipeline must be eliminated, but first we must be able to tell the difference between the two. I will call this the elephant in the classroom.

CHAPTER 34

MESSAGE TO ROLE MODELS

This is a very noble position that should never be taken lightly. When young men and women trust you it is a great responsibility that one should never take for granted. I honor those who take time out of their busy lives to teach, spend time, advise, and guide young urbanites. Inner city youth are very vulnerable due to their domestic, academic, and financial situations so they will always cherish any guiding light that enters their lives. As a role model, you are being watched by more youth than you could possibly imagine, including the ones that you have never had any contact or prior relationship with. You are actually being stalked on the down low. Everything you say and do is being watched and listened to. The way you walk, the way you dress, and the car you drive is secretly if not openly being admired by youth who need you. You are a father figure or a mother figure whether you like it or not. You are a light worker brought to this planet to guide our youth through the darkness. Do not assume that all of our young ones want to be gangsters, pimps, hustlers, strippers, or even rappers. These options are just the ones made readily available. Our youth aspire to be much more in their pursuit of knowledge, wealth, and greatness. Sometimes in the life of our youth, there are a few births that take place, a physical birth, which gets you onto the planet. This is usually the end of the mission for the biological parents whom for some reason or another are unable to provide anything more than a doorway to the physical world. True role models usually take the realms from there to physically raise the child into a young adult. So it is not uncommon for urban youth to have three or four sets of parents. The biological ones are the light in which they rode in on, and then there are the external lights that help guide as well. There may also be a set of "parents" to mentally raise a child, as well as a set to spiritually raise a child. This is the urban meaning of it takes a village. Ideally you would love for your physical parents to provide all of the guidance that one may need, but when that is not possible, there are always true roles models that serve as parents on another level.

Now that we have honored the angels, or angles (light), lets turn our attention towards the demons. These are the ones who prey on our youth for various reasons. The most common reason is to exploit them sexually. These are the false light bearers who always migrate to where unsupervised children reside, which in most cases is urban America. They appear to be righteous, always volunteering to help, and once they gain your trust you will be violated in the worse way. They are always looking for the troubled child who is also a loner. These demons are all around us. Everyone around children should be questioned and screened. I don't care how popular they appear to be. These are not the shining lights that brighten up our youth's lives, these are the ones who cast dark shadows and destroys futures. There was a time when we only had to focus on male predators, now you have to watch the females just as much as the males. So let the light workers work their magic, and let's continue to expose the demons that look to devour our seeds by protecting every child that may need our help. This is the Black Dot, and I am a role model.

CHAPTER 35

MESSAGE TO POLICE OFFICERS

The basic concept of the elephant in the room are major issues that everyone knows are true and need to be dealt with yet refuse to address. The more one refuses to address them (issues), the bigger the elephant becomes. This could not be more evident than the relationship between the police and urban communities across the country. Most white police officers are not only racist, but they also hate their jobs. They only took the position because they failed at everything else that they attempted to achieve in life. They never reached their aspirations to become a doctor, lawyer, or investment banker. So they settled. Let's face it; being a police officer is very low on the totem pole in white society. It is a glorified babysitting position for the white establishment. They are the ones on the frontline keeping the divide between white people who have attained a little more prosperity, and everyone else that are in pursuit of it. However, being a police officer does ensure that no matter what, at least you are still above black people. It means that you are still in a position of authority and can exercise that authority at any time and by any means. I do not want to hear about how noble and honorable the position is when their actions demonstrate the exact opposite. When those who have been ordained to serve and protect us do not even respect us, then the results are always going to be what we are seeing today regarding policing urban communities. These may sound like harsh words regarding the police, but this is how they are perceived through the minds eye of urban America. Now does this mean that there are not some white police officers that truly respect our community, and take their job seriously about protecting and serving those in need? Of course there are, but they are few and far in between. They can't help but be overwhelmed by the groupthink mentality of the majority, and the majority has a disdain for us, and our way of life. To white America, they are brave and courageous. It's just a matter of perspective. To travel from their homes everyday to guard the perimeters of the suburbs from urban America as if we are some caged animals is brave and courageous, to white people. Because of their treatment and rogue behavior towards urbanites, they are the open enemy. Again, this is a matter of perspective.

With that being said, I do believe that most police officers should be paid more money. I believe that the level of corruption that runs through the department, and their disdain for us would diminish tremendously. It will not eliminate racism altogether, but a lot of their disdain is based on pure jealousy. Imagine what goes through the mind of an officer who pulls over a young hustler driving a two hundred thousand dollar car for a mere traffic infraction, and the hustler is laughing at him because he knows the officer could never afford the car he driving. Or how about when he encounters a big time rapper that makes ten times what he does in one night, or how about the multimillionaire athlete who just dropped sixty thousand on the floor of a strip club. All of his life, he was taught that he was better than these so called animals that he has been sent to "protect" and here they are living a life that he could only dream of. This has to have an affect on the psyche of an officer. So instead of turning in the drugs from a bust, they hire the same people that they are suppose to arrest to resell them. Or instead of arresting the ones selling drugs and destroying the neighborhood, they extort them for police protection. At minimum, they stalk and harass famous athletes, hustlers, and rappers just for being richer than they will ever be. If they were paid better, I believe that our lives in the hood would be better. Of course this would not totally eliminate racism on the force because that is something that they have inherited for generations. Their fathers and grandfathers were officers of the law who shared the same racist views that they do. It's not just police officers; the entire system is corrupt and racist. It's just that we deal directly with the police since they are on the frontline so they get the brunt of our frustration. There is simply no other way to address this than to call it for what it is; most white police officers do not like black people, even the ones that they work with!

There is a brotherhood within the brotherhood within the police department. Black officers, who know and understand our experience first hand, soon suffer from the affects of the unified field of thought. They begin to view us as the enemy because of their allegiance to their job, and unfortunately to the authority of the force. There is nothing worse than encountering a black police officer accompanied by a white superior officer who treats us like animals without any remorse. Meanwhile, the white officers have their own crew that will never truly accept black officers in their inner circle. So urbanites truly feel no different when being stopped by a black officer or a white officer. That's the scary part of it. The biggest gangs in America are the police departments, and they are filled with black, white, Spanish, and many other denominations. However, at the top of the hierarchy was still white ruler-ship. This is a unique way to mask the overt racism within every police department. Make it appear that the department is diversified. The ruling body will always be Caucasian. In order to make real change within the department, there has to be a real shift in power. Until then, the overseer/slave mentality will continue to persist in the form of officer/black criminal reality.

How often have you heard of a black officer shooting an unarmed white teenager, or mistakenly killing a white off duty cop? You never hear of such incidents happening, why? Is it because white supremacy is so ingrained in the brain of black people that not even those in a position of authority would ever make such a mistake? Or are we conditioned to think that white people would never commit such crimes that would warrant such a response from a black officer? On the other hand, how many times have white police officers shot and killed unarmed black teens, or even shot black officers to death that weren't in uniform? These cases are too many to count. What's the difference in these scenarios? If you ask me, it looks like racism, period. White officers know that they would likely never be brought to justice for killing an unarmed black person. They may be charged but most likely will never be convicted. These are facts that I am stating, and if you have been following the news lately, you know that I am telling the absolute truth. White officers only have to use the magic code which is "I felt like my life was in danger", then a jury of their peers will have sympathy for the noble and courageous job that they do everyday by putting their lives on the line, and find them not guilty. Remember, it's a jury of their peers, not the victim's. The problem is systemic. As I previously mentioned in an earlier chapter, the overseer/officer dynamic is one that has been put in place to protect white interest, and property as well. Nowadays, the officer's job is to write as many tickets as possible to generate money for the city and state. This, along with the stop and search program being operated around the country keeps poor, inner city people on edge. This only adds to the heightened anxiety that already exist between urban communities and the police. When you are taxing the poor, you are asking for war! Do not think for a second, that what was taking place in Ferguson, Mo., is an isolated incident. Police departments all over the country are issuing summonses to poor people at an alarming rate. Consequently, most people who cannot afford to pay will wind up in the system, which will eventually lead to more fines and summonses. After being ticketed by a racist cop, we have to go in front of a racist judge to dispute the charges. This is why we hate authority, because it is rarely in our favor. What does white America think is going to happen if the urban community continues to be taxed heavily for no apparent reason, along with turning on the television and seeing their peers being gunned down in cold blood? Or is that the plan so that martial law will finally be implemented in this country. I can't remember at time when so many officers of the law blatantly committed so many heinous crimes against humanity. Makes me wonder what's really going on.

Here is my message to police officers. I believe that white officers should only police white neighborhoods from now on. This will immediately eliminate shooting unarmed black teens. White officers will never, and I mean never shoot unarmed white teens. There is the huge misnomer that white people do not commit crimes. Not only do they commit crimes, they commit them at an alarming rate. However, there has never been a phrase coined by the media called white on white crime. If you live in an all white neighborhood and you commit a crime in your neighborhood, what other type of crime would it be called? The stress and disdain that white officers feel for us would be gone. They would be in an environment that they are comfortable being in, dealing with a people that they are familiar with. This would lead to truly serving the community. White officers understand white culture. White officers would no longer fear for their lives. They would be governing the very communities that they live in so community relations would be better. They would know every child personally, even the troubled ones. They could become role models for young children in their neighborhoods. This would undoubtedly lead to a reduction in crime, and there would never be an us against them mentality. The job would become prestigious because you are protecting your own people in your own community. This would never happen because there is a violent nature about certain white males that needs to be openly expressed, and they would never exert that type of negative energy on their own. However, a lot of our race relation issues would be solve with this simple method.

The same could be said about black police officers governing their own communities. If every ranking officer, from top to bottom were black, the tensions in our neighborhoods would be reduced drastically. When I see completely black, I mean no white overseers, period. There would be no cultural divide. Most black officers come from the same neighborhoods that they would be patrolling. They no firsthand what the urban experience is about. They could run up on a bunch of black teens hanging in a tenement building and never feel threatened to the point where they have to pull their gun. Consequently there would be no "accidental" killings. He too would garner the respect of his neighborhood by being honorable in his approach to the job. He would not be pressure into treating his own people like savages to impress his white counterpart. He would immediately recognize that when we start talking with our hands in a flailing manner that this is just a form of expression used by urban youth when they are being animated, and not as a violent gesture that would warrant drawing a weapon. When you understand the culture, your mind is at ease. There is another misnomer that we in the urban communities do not want criminals brought to justice, that we are in favor of crime running rampant. We too want to live in communities where our children can go outside and play. We too want to live in communities where our elderly are safe. Yet when this is being executed by white officers who we know in our heart see all of us as criminals and treat us as such, this is a major problem. Integration may have been the worse thing that ever happened to people of color in this country because we stop learning how to do things for ourselves. We became dependent on a system that was never in our favor. Let's re-segregate, starting with the police departments first.

Newsflash, all white police officers are not racist, and all black people are not criminals. But when facing each other it's hard to differentiate between the two. So we act on the stereotypes fostered about each other. The truth of the matter is some of our people need to be arrested and placed in prison. Yeah, I said it. Have you seen worldstarhiphop.com lately? Have you seen the way that we act? No, we can't blame it all on racism and white supremacy. If I didn't know our worth, I would think that black people were violent savages who hated their women. So when a police officer sees this because they watch Worldstar, too, how do you expect them to respond to us when the see us in our communities? Just as equally, there are super racist cops who are also Klansmen who are on a mission to take out as many black people as possible, no matter innocent or not. It is there duty to the brotherhood to do so. This is the current situation being faced by officers and innocent urbanites alike. We have to be able to conduct ourselves accordingly, and racist officers have to be exposed and flush out in order to add balance to our societies and communities. We are all at fault for what our communities have become. Everyone needs to be held to a much higher standard. Police officers need to develop a respect for humanity, and we need to rise above the obstacles created to hinder us and develop an overall respect for ourselves. Then and only then will true change come to urban America and America as a whole.

CHAPTER 36

MESSAGE TO PASTORS AND REVERENDS

Most pastors and reverends are out of touch with anything that is not related to Christianity. So their approach to reach the youth is through a book that was not only given to them by our open enemy, but was beaten and tortured into them. I understand the significance of Christianity getting us through a tough time during slavery. I also understand how it has affected the psyche of our ancestors who had nothing else to hold on to after being robbed of their culture. So I do not want to disrespect my elders who used Christianity as a form of spiritual shelter to carry our people through the storm to help us survive. However, we also ate pig's feet and cow ass to nourish our bodies and survive as well. As our understanding of the dangers of eating in such a manner grew, along with better options being made available, most of our elders made healthier choices. When we know better, we have to do better. This new generation knows better, even if they do not possess the mental capacity to do better. They do not want to eat pig's feet and cow's ass, just as they do not want to digest the spiritual equivalent. Just as police officers are on the frontline physically guarding the perimeters of our neighborhoods,

221

pastors and reverends are on the frontline monitoring our spiritual progress. Most of them know that you and I are not Christian by nature. They know that we have existed long before Christianity was ever created. Most of them know this because they are Masons, and in the lodge they are taught the truth about our history. So they have made a conscious effort to mislead you. I mean this when I say this: If you are a Christian and this is the faith that you follow, and you have followed it your entire life, and it has done some amazing things for you, and it has gotten you through tough times, I truly respect that. I know it might not sound like I do, but I really do. However, you cannot be a Christian and also complain about white supremacy at the same time. They are embedded within the very culture of each other. Or do you truly believe that Europeans beat, tortured, murdered, castrated, hung, raped, and divided us, but when it came to religion, they were honest and honorable? Really? You cannot separate the two, when you proudly say that I am a Christian, what you are saying is, "I proudly accept that fact that I am under European rule."

It's one thing to be under European rule and fighting everyday to free yourself and your people, and it is something totally different to accept it without any resistance. White supremacy takes attendance every Sunday afternoon, and as long as the numbers are strong, they know that their rule will continue. They know that as long as you are under spiritual lockdown, your mental and physical lockdown are a synch. The church has become the ultimate monitoring center, headed up by the pastor himself. Who are the first ones to come out and quell major disturbances whenever a crisis arises? Yet the pastor or reverend never step outside of the church to deal with any non-Christian related issues when there is no crisis. Please do not make mention of the two or three times a year that good ole Christian folk go feed the homeless to make themselves feel good about doing the lord's work. Right outside of every church is the stark reality of our situation. Most churches are government funded through the tax-exempt laws of 501c3 status. What this means in a nutshell is that most churches are under the authority of the government. Yet if the government as a whole is our enemy for the way that they treat our people, then what does that make the pastor or reverend? Hmmm. In this day and time, truth has become the enemy. Most of our people suffer from cognitive dissonance, which forces them to hold on to their beliefs even tighter when confronted with truth. Truth should make you very uncomfortable. If you are in constant agreement with your truth, then it's time for a new truth. The pursuance of truth should be a lifelong journey that takes you all over the place, physically, mentally, and of course spiritually. Truth should make you contradict yourself on a regular basis. Your perception of the truth should change based on your understanding of life itself.

Most people do not want the truth because the truth forces you to change your reality. Religious people find it the hardest to deal with truth; they rely on faith and their belief in their God. That supersedes truth. I have no problem with faith and belief, but your faith and belief should be upgraded every now and then to match the vibrations of what is really going on in the world. Instead, our people head to the church in droves to have their belief and faith in God restored, and right there to reassure them that whatever truths they have encountered outside of the church doesn't matter is the pastor or reverend. I can hear Christians screaming "not my pastor, not my church". Yeah, your pastor and your church, too. If my theory on cognitive dissonance is correct, then after reading this chapter, more people will be flocking to their local churches than ever before.

If you want to know about the unknown, you study the known. This is the method used by scientist to uncover mysteries and decode life. Well the known is our ancestors and elders who have put their faith in Christianity have been waiting and waiting and waiting for the return of a mystery God to save them. They have also been conditioned to believe that if they tolerate the abuse, discrimination, and racism of this world, that when they die the will be rewarded in the afterlife. The known is as of today, no savior has returned, and no elder had died and come back to verify such beliefs about the afterlife. It's hard to believe that in this day and time with so much information, data, and historical proof available that the majority of our people still believe such stories. That's the power of faith. However, if nothing changes, then nothing changes. We will continue to suffer at the hands of white supremacy. If your pastor is not teaching you that, "Ye are Gods, and the laws cannot be broken," if your pastor is not teaching you that, "The kingdom of heaven is within you," if your pastor is not teaching you the real reason that you worship on "Sun" day, and not "Son" day, if your pastor is not teaching you an African-based doctrine that glorifies your historical past that exist well beyond Christianity, then he or she is actually blocking your spiritual blessings. They may actually be sabotaging your path to true spirituality. There are some revolutionary pastors who have incorporated the African spiritual system into their teachings, and to them I say, thank you. My message to all other pastors who continue to follow the Christian tradition of rocking our people to sleep I say, "Let my people go!"

CHAPTER 37

MESSAGE TO COACHES

This is another crucial position in urban America that is often overlooked. A great coach is a father figure, guider, teacher, counselor, and the head of a soup kitchen if needed. He or she stands at the doorway of dreams when it comes to most inner city youth looking to use sports as their medium of expression, and their ticket out of the hood. Yet it is deeper than just coaching a sport, they are life coaches as well. Their input in the lives of these young men and women could be the difference between making it very far, or never getting up off the bench to even get into the game of life. It is for this reason that they are held to a very high standard, and most of them do live up to these expectations. Life is a game, and a great coach has the ability to draw on the similarities between the games that they coach and life itself. I am specifically talking about the frontline coaches who deal with the most dangerous, misguided youth in America, the ones who may have a little less talent, but a lot of hopes and dreams nonetheless. A coach is the first father to a lot of young men growing up without their biological ones around. It is the first time that most of them will ever be disciplined in their lives. It may even be the first time that they have to think of someone other than himself because most sports are team related. It is the first time that most of them will be held accountable for their actions. Coaches today have so much more that they have to deal with than ever before. They have to be abreast of the gang activity that goes on in the community, social media, ESPN, crazy parents who think their child is the next Michael Jordan, and a host of other things that are not technically sports related. Great coaches have to find a way to keep our youth motivated and focused. There is a lot of temptation growing up in the hood from hustlers, rappers, ballers, and drugs. Most coaches understand that there is a lot riding on a child's ability to play a sport. In most cases, the entire family is depending on it.

The poverty levels in urban America are so high, and the expectations for education are so low, yet these two mediums are intertwined. Back in the days, gifted athletes from the inner city who were basically illiterate were allowed to bypass the education system. They were given a pass. Nowadays this is regulated differently and these young men in particular have to at least pass standard test to be admitted to college. This creates an additional set of problems because the public school system is not suited to teach and get the best out of our children, yet they need it to pursue their dreams. So a coach's job is very hard. They have the arduous task of molding our young men into those with great character, get them to understand the importance of education, even if it's just a tool to reach a greater goal, and steer clear of the streets. Most coaches are underpaid and overworked. Their true reward comes from knowing that they played a major role in developing and guiding our youth to brighter futures. No amount of money can equate to the time, energy, effort, love, and support that a great coach can provide. I am speaking from personal experience. My summer league basketball and softball coaches saved my life. Not that I had aspirations of going pro, but I needed an outlet on a regular basis to keep me focused on something positive as opposed to all of the negative things that were going on domestically. So even for the young ones who are not that talented, sports and a great coach to teach it, is still viable. So I have nothing but respect for the coach/fathers who helped to mold and shelter me from the urban storm that could have easily swept me away.

There are a few more hats that coaches have to incorporate into their already busy repertoire; one is that of financial advisor. These youth are coming into money at an alarming rate and most of them could not balance a scale, let alone a checkbook. Not only do they need to understand the science of economics, but they must also be mentally prepared to recognize and fight off all of the wolves that await them in the real world of finance. The vultures come in all shapes and sizes so to speak and are not easily detected. Making it to the pros is only half the battle, and for those who are talented as our youth are, it is the easy half. Understanding how to save, invest, and prepare for the future is the hard half of the battle. If the coach himself is not well-versed in the understanding of economics, then he should hire someone to come in once a week and teach his young men and women how to maintain the lifestyle that they have worked so hard to achieve. There are investment bankers who would love to share their knowledge for free in most cases. Start by giving them all a theoretical million-dollar contract, and give them the tools to manage, budget, and save. If done correctly, this will show them that a million dollars is really not a lot of money when it has to last over a course of time. In the process, the coach can show them how to cut the weeds to reveal who the snakes are. Unless, of course, they are the snakes!

Not every coach is in it for the well being of the children. There are many who are only in it to benefit by pimping their youth to sneaker companies, collages, and other programs that are geared toward exploiting our babies, and believe me when I say there are a ton of them. The coach becomes the link between corporate America and urban America. For these coaches, there is no teaching beyond the physical aspect of the game and they usually are only interested in the very talented children. The coaches will even ship these children out of the hood to better schools and better basketball programs with the promise of a kickback once the player is signed to a sneaker deal or professional contract. They are motivated by greed. These are the youth who are most likely to wind up right back where they started because their coach didn't prepare them for life outside of the ball court. These coaches are very dangerous because they come under the guise of helping by providing sneakers and a little spending money up front. Little do most of our youth know that this is considered an investment in them that will be paid back exponentially when it's all said and done. I do not respect these types of coaches who are only in it to exploit our young men and women. Coaching is an honorable position that should be held in high regard. It should never be taken for granted or abused. My direct message to coaches is to honor our youth by guiding them from your heart. They will cherish you for the rest of their lives as being the ones who are solely responsible for their success.

CHAPTER 38

MESSAGE TO DOCTORS

It truly does take a village to raise a child. I have taken the liberty to list a few of the key players that I feel play a major role in the development of our youth from a community perspective. In urban America, the outside of the home may have a greater influence than what is going on inside of the home. There are a lot of intricate parts that assist in the success or failure of an inner city child, and this list would not be complete I didn't mention doctors. Today's doctors do nothing more than vaccinate and medicate our children at an alarming rate. Vaccinations have been linked to autism among other diseases. They are filled with a multitude of toxins that wouldn't be fit enough to give to an animal. Leading healthcare practitioners always refute the dangers of such vaccinations. This leaves most uneducated parents confused and pressured. So most parents buckle under the pressure and place their trust in the doctors. If something bad happens to the child as a result of being vaccinated, the doctor bears no responsibility. There is a disclaimer form floating around on the Internet that will place the power back into the hands of parents. It's a liability letter that basically states that if anything should happen to your child as a result of this experimental practice that they can and will be held liable for any damages. Most doctors will refuse to sign it because they know of the dangers. There is also a form that you can fill out that would make your child exempt from having to get these shots due to religious reasons. Anything that punctures the skin is considered experimental science and you have a right not to have your child experimented on. This information is only for the progressive parents who are not afraid to fight the system for the safety of their children. All others will succumb to the fear tactics of the doctors and nurses alike. Just as critical are the medications that are being heavily prescribed to our children. The most common drugs are Ritalin, Meyylin, Metadate, Concerta, and Daytrana. These drugs have our babies walking around in a comatose state. They are also very prone to violence. When this is coupled with the fact that most of our youth are also on alcohol or other illegal substances, the chemical mixture could lead to disaster. At minimum, they could wind up in some mental institution, or worse, in prison or dead. So it is illegal to self-medicate, but if the doctor prescribes something – that in most cases is far worse – then it's ok.

There is very little true diagnosis that is taking place in the hood, just prescriptions being written. As a result, the root causes of their illness are never addressed. Most of these doctors are in it for the profits and nothing else. There are also so far out of touch with what real healing is all about. They have been trained to only deal with the affects of an illness and not the cause, so they never truly get to the root of any problem. They are worse than the drug dealers on the street corner. The only difference is that they have a license to sell drugs and the average street hustler does not. They make millions of dollars by prescribing certain drugs by certain companies. Kickbacks become their primary incentive. The morals of being a doctor should never be compromised, especially not at risk of our children's well being.

Doctors have their own secret society. The Hippocratic oath taken by them buys their allegiance to a system that keeps the public in the dark about what truly goes on in the medical field, and behind closed doors. On the surface, this oath is about being ethical and upright when dealing with patients, but I beg to differ. True healing requires an understanding that goes far beyond medicine. Holistic health is the study of mind, body, and soul. In order to heal the body, you must first heal the mind. To heal the mind you must first heal the soul. Everything is connected to everything. This is the science of metaphysics. It deals with the cause of disease, not just the affects. Science itself is beginning to catch up with the world of metaphysics. Stay away from the hospital and their doctors at all cost. Find yourself a great holistic practitioner that will teach you all about preventive measures, unless you are in need of immediate medical attention for bleeding or some other traumatic situation. These doctor are not your friends or allies. They are here to make a profit and nothing else. Perhaps it didn't always start out like that, some doctors became such to truly help people, but the system as a whole is corrupt, so slowly but surely, they too found themselves just pushing products that the pharmaceutical companies create for larger profits and gains. Most doctors are like robots, you come into their office, they give you a quick diagnosis, they look in their medical book for the matching prescription, and they prescribe it and send you home. Doctors should be arrested for recommending milk, cheese, butter, and eggs as a part of a balance diet. This is difficult for most parents to understand since they get this stuff for free, in most cases directly from the doctor. Only in America are doctors just as sick as their patients.

Dr. Oz, who has a television show about health on the Fox network, recently came under scrutiny by his own peers for teaching people some alternative methods of healing themselves by using herbs, meditation, and other natural remedies. In their eyes, he broke the Hippocratic oath. He understands the need for us to change our thinking and perspective when it comes to health if we are to survive. I give him credit for being brave enough to challenge the very philosophy of the field in which he was trained in to help people. That is what being a doctor is truly all about. Stop pushing poison to our communities. Stop using your position of authority to undermine the poor. Stop misdiagnosing people for financial gain. Stop relying on old medical practices to treat modern issues. Doctors need to become a part of the solutions as opposed to being a part of the problem. I salute the doctors who are brave enough to think outside of the box, and the ones who are not all about financial gains. I salute the ones who truly understand how critical it is for our youth to have great physical, mental, and spiritual health. We must heal as a community. Everyone has an equal role to play if we are to uplift our community and prepare for the future. In the future, doctors have to earn our trust by understanding who we are as a people. Our elders didn't deal with the affects of our illness; they went straight to the cause. We are at war socially, politically, economically, spiritually, and medically. If you are not with the people, then you are against the people. It is just that simple.

CHAPTER 39

MESSAGE TO GANGS

George Zimmerman is still walking around freely and the police are still gunning down our brothers and sisters daily. So what does that say about how thorough your gang is, or how your team will buss shots against anyone, or how feared your crew is? It's amazing how quick our young bangers will dole out street justice to those who look just like them, but will ignore the injustices that are perpetrated against them by those who do not look like them. The penalty for the crime is the same, yet the rate in which we violate each other is far greater than crimes against corrupt police officers or those who come into our communities and violate our children and women. In the eyes of authority, you are a joke. In fact, you work for the authorities. If you don't believe me, let's assess the situation. Who are you selling drugs to? Who are you having shoot-outs against? What neighborhoods are you terrorizing? How are the drugs getting into our neighborhoods? Who's manufacturing the guns? Who is directly responsible for policing our communities? When you do the work of our oppressors, you become our oppressors. Our children cannot walk the streets, not because of racist white people, but because of the fear that they have of those who look just like them. Our elderly live in constant fear of the ones who should respect and revere them the most: our youth. Our women feel unprotected and, in some cases, violated by the very men who should be honoring them at all costs. These are any community's most valuable possessions: its children, women, and elderly. It is the responsibility of every man in our community to honor this code of protection. Gangs are supposed to be our frontline of defense, not the ones who are keeping us sealed in and contained. However, the origins of gangs back in the day had a different mission than they do now. A gang's number one priority was to protect their neighborhoods from outside invaders. Those outside invaders included corrupt police officers that had no respect for us as a people, as well as those who looked just like us but were a danger to us.

There was a code of ethics, even on the streets that was followed to ensure the safety of the community first. Once guns and drugs were introduced, the mission quickly became about money, power, and territory. Or should I say, the illusion of money, power, and territory. The money is not worth the paper that it is printed on. How many gang members have an 800 credit score, or actual property, or gold? And I don't want to hear the excuse that gangs deal in illegal activity. So does the government! If you cannot sit down with your elected officials and have bills passed in favor of your community, you have no power. As far as territory is concerned, do you really think you own that block that you sell drugs on? As soon as a few well-to-do white families decide to move into your neighborhood – as they are often doing these days – your so-called block is no longer yours. You can bet your life on it. And I am absolutely tired of hearing that the reason we destroy our own communities is because of racism and white supremacy. Sure, if you want to get ultra technical, we can trace it all back to that in some shape, form, or fashion. Yet, our people suffer heavy from victim consciousness. By blaming white people for all of the things that are wrong with us, it gives us a built-in excuse to not try to overcome these obstacles. Why should our youth try to clean themselves up when the end results will always be the same? As long as the problems exist outside of our own doing, we don't have to accept responsibility for anything regarding our own resurrection. Wake up people! We have to accept responsibility for our own destiny, starting with our gangs. They need to be upgraded.

I have often said that a lot of these gang members are warrior spirits who chose to reincarnate at this time to help us fight our open enemy. However, since we have not engaged our open enemy, or made it crystal clear by our own actions who that open enemy is, they have begun to stage war against themselves. Imagine being a warrior with no war to fight. More importantly, since we suffer from victim consciousness, the very warriors who were sent here to help us are victimizing us instead. What did you expect? We are the ones who summoned them, so we have to suffer the consequences. We know and understand that gangs became possible due to the lack of fathers and positives males in the home. The broken family structure led to males in particular looking for family outside of the home. In the interest of time and space, I am not going to do an entire psychoanalysis into gangs and their affects on our communities. But I will say this: When a culture begins to turn on itself, the end of that culture is eminent. We have to give our young man and women new direction, including gangs. The only drugs or so called drugs that they should be selling from now on is marijuana. With the ever-changing laws that are now in their favor, marijuana could be a lucrative business venture with no casualties. There will be no need to kill each other anymore because there will be enough proceeds to go around, and soon it will all be legal. Take a look at what is going on in Denver and Seattle. Then we need our elders to convince them to put some of this money to use in a political capacity as well as in other ways to strengthen our communities. See, the truth of the matter is, if they had a viable source of income and also felt useful to their communities, I believe that they would be willing to make change. It is our responsibility to give them purpose. Are far as gunplay is concerned, every member of a gang should be required to spend a certain amount of hours at a gun range to work on their accuracy and understand the science of fire arms, as well as the science of urban warfare. This will cut down on innocent people being struck down and prepare them for war should it ever be necessary. Do not think for a minute that the militia are not sharp shooters and highly skilled in warfare.

Knowledge of self is the most important tool that we can arm them with. They need to be taught who they are. They are the guardians of our community; they just don't know it yet. Too often we condemn our youth for their faults but we do not show them the potential of their greatness. At the end of the day, they are our babies. With a legitimate economic foundation, the proper training in urban warfare, and knowledge of self, we can turn any gang into an asset. We have to make them an extension of our family. This will not be easy to do since most of these gangs are filled with government agents and informants. If we do not have an army, then we do not have a nation. Who is more qualified at this moment in the hood to lead an army? Who has at least some experience with firing weapons? Who in the hood has the keen eye to detect enemy forces on the move? Who is built to stand on our urban corners in any weather? Who can generate hundreds of thousands, if not millions of dollars for food, supplies, and more weapons? The answer to these questions is Gangs. Yet with no direction or purpose, the guns are pointed at us, the resources are being robbed from us, and we are prisoners in our own homes, and they are not afraid to die, they prove it everyday. Remember, the police department was a gang first, so was the fire department as well. They understood the importance of unionizing, politics, and economics. Now the run the biggest gangs in the country.

CHAPTER 40

MESSAGE TO ELDERS

Forgive our youth for not having the knowledge of their true history since it's not being taught to them in the public school system, and we haven't provided an alternative method of educating them. Forgive them for not having the utmost respect for women since all of the older men that they look up to, rappers, athletes, and actors all have multiple women, call them out of their names, or prefer strippers instead. Please forgive them for being so violent since there are no jobs or positive outlets, but plenty of drugs and guns made readily available for them to indulge in. forgive them for not respecting their elders since most of their elders have disowned them, pointed fingers at them, or blame them for everything that is wrong with society. Forgive our youth for looking up to rappers and hustlers, yet these are the only ones who respect them by telling their story in a manner in which they can truly relate. Forgive our youth for dating white women when all of their prominent role models for over the last fifty years have married white women once they reached a certain level of success. Forgive our youth for being gay since no one taught them their true culture and they have adopted the culture of their oppressor. Forgive our youth for acting like savages when they were left to fend for themselves, with no mothers and fathers to guide them, a police system that is out to arrest or kill them, a court system that is not in their favor, a prison system that capitalizes off of their slave labor, and a workforce that will not hire them. Forgive our youth for feeling abandoned by their own elders who let all of this happen on their watch.

This younger generation is the byproduct of integration, the crack era, and popular culture. This mixture, along with social media, has created a generation that is almost unrecognizable to our elders. However, at their core, they are still we. While most of what our elders endured was physical and mental, our youth have endured a psychological beat-down like none that we have witnessed before. As a result, they have morphed into the most dangerous, violent, sexually active, drug using, rebellious generation of all time. Integration forced them to lose the little bit of identity that they had left. At least during segregation, we demonstrated a sense of self- pride, an entrepreneurial spirit, and a cultural identity. In a society that is predominantly European, it is hard to hold on to your cultural values when we are being forced to mix with others. The crack era opened the floodgates for murder, money, and mayhem. Those who wouldn't normally have the heart to commit murder were doing so at an alarming rate. The stakes were too high. Women who wouldn't normally perform sex acts were doing so frequently. The notion of being nude in public became secondary to getting a hit of crack. This led to the whole stripper culture being so readily accepted in the years to come. The hood had never seen so much money and opportunity before. Even those who had foresight and vision capitalized off of the crack era by starting legit businesses off of the proceeds. The children who were birthed during this time period were of the unified field of thought of that time period. The thought process of that time period was, I will do anything for this money, I will even shoot up my own neighborhoods for this money,

I will even kill my own brother for this money, I will sell to children, pregnant women, and elders. This mindset altered the very DNA of the generation that we see today. This also led to the increased hostility between the police and our urban community because these crack dealers were even willing to shoot it out with law enforcement for that money. No one saw this epidemic coming except president Ronald Reagan, and the C.I.A., headed up by George W. Bush, who allowed it to happen on their watch as a part of the Iran/Contra affairs. So I cannot put all of the blame on our elders for such a shift in consciousness.

Just think back 5 years B.C. (before crack) at the state of our people, and tell me that what we see today is not a direct result of crack cocaine. I call it crack because it cracked the code of our DNA like no other drug before it. All other drugs before it like heroin, marijuana, PCP, etc. all allowed us to maintain the essence of who we were. Crack created an entire new species altogether, the soulless generation. We always claim that this generation is so quick to sell their souls for fame and fortune, when the truth of the matter is they never had a soul to begin with. They are hardwired to pursue fame and fortune. In fact, they look at you strange if you do not do the same. When Hip Hop was replaced with Rap, this led to our entry into POP culture. POP culture has become one world culture where every culture is meshed into one. Rappers are known by politicians, politicians are known by athletes, athletes are known by actors, actors are known by "ballers", "ballers are known by wall street investors, wall street investors are known by strippers, strippers are known by rappers. This one world culture has stripped our youth of any and everything connected to their ancestral bloodline. They are now of the get money culture, the gay culture, the transplant culture, the stripper culture, the killer culture, and more.

Our elders have to take a different approach to reach and save our youth. They can no longer hold them to the same standards as they previously held for themselves. They have to come off of their high horse and walk amongst the people once again. They have to take all that they have learned and integrate it into what is going on today. They have to almost work in reverse, build a stairway, not from the top down as if from a higher plane of existence to that of a lower realm, but from the bottom up as if they are building a stairway to heaven for all that wish to climb it. They have to rewrite the code of this particular matrix. The old paradigm, which they know and love, may be gone forever. Those elders who choose to live in a bubble of our ancestors past, and do things the old way may not make it. We are the vanguards of a new culture in which the history is yet to be written. Those of use who are not yet elders, but too old to be considered youth have to bridge the gap between the youth and our elders. We have to transcribe the ancient text into text messages if need be. We have to codify the old teachings into the current matrix of language used by our youth. We have to use the science of art for what it was truly meant for, which is to uplift our humanity through sound, visuals, dance, storytelling, and spirit. We are the ones who we have been waiting for. Once our elders recognize the true potential of our youth, they will be more than willing to assist in ushering in a new paradigm because the future of our people are depending on it.

CHAPTER 41

CONCLUSION

This is truly the dawn of a new day. Our youth have become the agents of chaos sent here not to restore order but to usher in a new order. This new order will look like chaos to those who are holding up the old establishment that has been detrimental to so many for so long. Why restore that which has hindered the growth, progress, and ascension of our people? The media has portrayed the recent unrest in urban cities around the country as a tragedy because so-called "thugs" were looting and burning down their own establishments. Nothing could be further from the truth. We don't own anything in our own communities so we are not emotionally attached to it. If it would bring about real change in this country we would watch it all burn to the ground. The hypocrisy in it all is that America was birthed on looting, murder, theft, disease, and deception. We presently travel to other countries to loot, murder and steal their resources and are called patriots for doing so, but when its citizens fight for the same rights, they are called thugs or, even worse, terrorists. Even more surprising is the response by many well-to-do "black' athletes, ministers, actors, and entertainers who criticize our youth by calling them savages and stating that this was not the way to go about bringing real change in this country. Well, what is the way? Every time that they rely on the justice system to be fair and balanced, they are heavily disappointed. Justice is supposed to be blind, but even when she can "see", via the many cell phone videos of corrupt police officers committing crimes against our youth, she continues to look the other way. Most oppressed people in this country don't want change. They just want to make a piece of change, so they will fight to keep the current structure in place under the guise of the many opportunities that are available if you just work hard and don't complain. In our youth, we are witnessing the rebel in us that has been lost due to conformity. In our youth we are witnessing the bold, brave, and courageousness in us that has abandoned us due to docility. We have been doing the same things for so long that change has become the enemy. As a result, we look at our youth as our enemy when in fact; all that they are doing is forging change. Even President Obama stated, "Change has come to America." I'm not sure if this was the change that he envisioned, but he was right.

We are not victims. We are the beneficiaries of over four hundred years of a beautiful struggle. Our enemies' attempt to break our spirit has done the exact opposite. We rise in spite of slavery, we rise in spite of being tortured, we rise in spite of being castrated, we rise in spite of losing our culture, religion, language, and God, we rise in spite of racism, we rise in spite of discrimination, we rise in spite of police brutality, and in the words of the late, great Maya Angelou, "and still we rise"! How can we not be the chosen people? Who else has gone through anything remotely close to what we have endured? We are the most talented, gifted, and spiritual people on the planet. Who has produced the greatest athletes in the world? Who has produced the greatest musicians in the world? Who has produced the greatest thinkers in the world? Urban America is the trendsetters for the entire planet. The world sees in us what we rarely see in our selves: courage, bravery, brilliance, resilience, and fortitude. Most people would hate to admit it, but we have the beautiful struggle to thank for our ascension into greatness. The diamond within us shines bright.

If you believe that we will one day live in a world with no racism, no police brutality, no homosexuality, with black people all over the world uniting under one super Black Power movement, you are delusional. If you believe that we will one day live in a utopia where there are no drugs and alcohol, no sexual predators, no crime, and we, the original people will reclaim our throne because Europeans have agreed to relinquish their power, you are super delusional. This type of thinking only demonstrates how out of touch we are with reality as it is currently being broadcast, and how far we have delved into a form of mental sickness that we may never recover from. I wrote this book to upgrade the operating system of parents, teachers, and elders. This physical, mental, and spiritual software update is the direct result of studying the ways and actions of our youth. While I physically wrote the book, I am only reporting and recording my findings based on the everyday life and struggle of our youth in this paradigm, even though it is written in the first person. In order to write a book of this magnitude, I had to suspend my own racist, homophobic, pro militant, pro Black thought process, and become just an observer. What I observed is that our youth do not see the world through the same lens as I and many others who were brought up and conditioned to think a certain way regarding these issues do. Sure, they recognize that these issues exist, but they will not allow themselves to be hindered or held back because of all of the toxic energy geared toward them to stop them from ascending. That's the difference between them and us.

This generation speaks the universal language of Hip Hop. There is a variation of the language being spoken everywhere on the planet. So wherever I go, if they speak Hip Hop, I am welcomed. This is huge. According to a recent report out of the University of London, Hip Hop music is the pinnacle of music in the last 50 years. It has had a greater impact than even the Beatles. History will soon recognize Hip Hop as a civilization! I opened this book stressing the importance of Hip Hop to parents, teachers, and elders. If you do not have at least a general understanding of the culture, then you have no chance of communicating with this generation. Hip Hop runs through the veins of our youth. It is their birthright. Hip Hop is forever. As long as there is a heartbeat, there will be a drum. As long as there is an ability to speak, there will be the spoken word. As long as we have hands, there will be symbols, glyphs, and signs. As long as there are physical bodies, there will be a temple for Hip Hop to be housed in. And as long as we have a mind, Hip Hop's potential will be infinite. We are just beginning to scratch the surface of the metaphysical principles of Hip Hop. The exoteric understanding enables us to express the outer energy of the culture through dance, song, writings, and word. The esoteric understanding opens us up to our true spiritual potential, and unlocks the code of life itself. The urban experience has created the perfect climate, and provided us with the hidden elixir needed to perform the necessary alchemical rituals to bring Hip Hop into existence, and, in doing so, transform man into God.

In closing, allow me to say this: Yes, we are the original Jewish people who were stolen from West Africa. Yes, we are the Moors who ruled Spain for hundreds of years. Yes, we the original founders of the Islamic faith. Yes, we are the high priests from the Congo. Yes, we are the indigenous people who occupied North America long before the European was even a thought. And, yes, we are the great ones who placed the pyramids on Mars. Yes, we are the ascendants of all of the above, even though it is hard to recognize us with our pants hanging off of our butts and we carry semi-automatic weapons, sell drugs, murder each other, disrespect our women, and act as if we have no idea of our great lineage. However, at second glance, if you look close enough with your first eye, you can still see the greatness that we possess. We still rule empires. Have you heard of Barack Obama? We still hold positions of royalty. Have you ever heard of King James? By the way, he can fly! We are still keepers of the pyramids. Have you ever heard of Jay Z? Our women are still the nurturers and healers of the planet, and have amassed great fortunes doing so. Have you ever heard of Oprah Winfrey? We still have the greatest mathematicians that the world has ever produced. Have you ever heard of Gabriel Oyibo? He cracked the code the Albert Einstein could not in his body of work titled " The Grand Unified Theorem. We still have great astrophysicists. Have you ever heard of Neil deGrasse Tyson? We still produce great musicians who have the power to use their words to heal and uplift humanity. Have you ever heard of Stevie Wonder? We still have great ones amongst us who have the power to unify all of the Gods, religions and sciences under one culture. Have you ever heard of Afrika Bambaataa? There is no one coming to save us. We are already here. This is ancient KMT. We are the historical figures that they will speak about in the future. Yes, we drink, smoke, party, and celebrate the ancestors like most would never understand, but we still hold the key to humanities survival. In our youth, we see all that was, all that is, and all that will be, so let's embrace them on their journey. With that said,

"This is The Black Dot,
These are my chronicles,
This is my story,
and I'm sticking to it.

Peace!